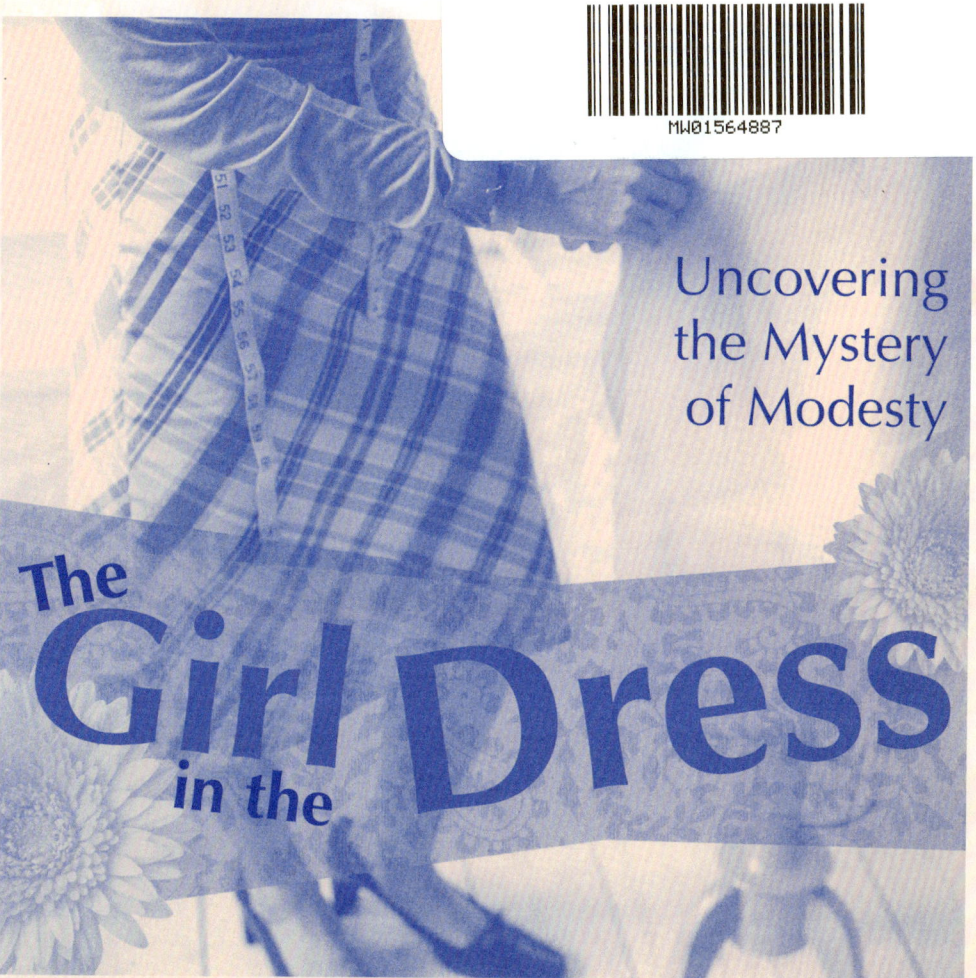

The Girl in the Dress
Uncovering the Mystery of Modesty

The Girl in the Dress

Uncovering the Mystery of Modesty

by Lori Wagner
with Gwyn Oakes, Mary Loudermilk
and Marjorie Kinnee

The Girl in the Dress
Uncovering the Mystery of Modesty

by Lori Wagner
    with Gwyn Oakes, Mary Loudermilk and Marjorie Kinnee

© 2009 Ladies Ministries, UPCI

Cover and Interior Design: Laura Jurek

Bible translations used: Unless otherwise noted, the King James Version is the primary Bible translation used. Also included for reference are the New King James Version, New International Version, and New American Standard Bible.

All rights reserved. No portion of this publication may be reproduced, stored in an electronic system, or transmitted in any form or by any means, electronic, mechanical, photocopy, recording, or otherwise, without the prior permission of the author(s). Brief quotations may be used in literary reviews.

Printed in United States of America

A *More to Life* Publication
8855 Dunn Road
Hazelwood, MO 63042

Table of Contents

Acknowledgments 7

Foreword 9

Introduction: The Girl in the Mirror 11

Chapter One: Who Am I? 15

Chapter Two: God's Design 29

Chapter Three: Falling in Love 47

Chapter Four: Inside Out 63

Chapter Five: Does God Care about What You Wear? 79

Chapter Six: Fashion Statements 105

Chapter Seven: The Mystery of Modesty and
   the Protective Power of Purity 125

Notes & Resources 137

Acknowledgments

Thank you to all who contributed to *The Girl in the Dress*, with special recognition to:

Gayla Baughman
Anuhea Drummondo
Angela Harwood
Cindy Meadows
Marcia Jackson
Geanice Langley
Julie Long
Amber Otwell
Bonnie Peacock
Marlissa Prince
Anne Richardson
Gail Snyder
Claudette Walker
Marvin Walker
All the members of the Pure Path group

Foreword

How exciting!
Finally, a book written just for girls—
a book about the importance and beauty of holiness.

The Girl in the Dress helps us to realize why it is important to take a stand in today's world on modesty and purity. There is no need to hang our heads in embarrassment about who we are. Lori Wagner and the writing team take an excellent approach concerning the way the Bible teaches us to walk, talk, and dress.

Young people in the world go to great lengths to stand out and be different. They will wear all black, dye their hair blue, pink, or purple and wear clothes that are ripped on purpose—just to be unique. How blessed we are to learn that I Peter 2:9 says, "But ye are a chosen generation, a royal priesthood, an holy nation, a **peculiar** people." (Yay! We're different!) What is the purpose of being different? "That ye should shew forth the praises of him who hath called you out of darkness into his marvelous light."

Girls, I think it is time that we let His marvelous light shine through us. As we live and dress according to the Word of God, our inner beauty will take over and the outward result will be one that makes us *truly* beautiful. Shine on!

Debbie Sanders
Director of Today's Christian Girl

The Girl in the Mirror

"I disagree totally. It doesn't matter what I wear!" Jackie sucked in her stomach and pulled up the zipper of her new mermaid skirt. "Anyway, you know what the Bible says. God isn't looking at my outside. He's looking at my heart!" Jackie tugged at the snug fabric hugging her hips until the hem of her skirt inched down to mid-knee. "There. See? It's almost below my knees. Nobody can complain about *this* skirt."

Katelyn watched as Jackie pulled a form-fitting t-shirt from her drawer and stretched it over a molded demi bra, the undergarment's outline clearly revealed by the tightly-drawn knit fabric. Pulling some heels from the closet, she slipped them on and finished off her outfit with a clanky silver belt riding low on her hips. Jackie walked a few steps away from the full-length mirror, turned, and checked her reflection.

Speechless, Katelyn took everything in. Her eyes focused unconsciously on her friend's magnetic, belted hips swaying with each step. When she realized she was staring, Katelyn forced her gaze away, but the next place that immediately drew her attention was the outline of Jackie's protruding chest. "Oh, my," Katelyn thought to herself. "I'm a girl, and if I can't help noticing body parts in this outfit, what are the guys going to think when they look at her?" Jackie turned sideways before the mirror, every curve of her feminine shape, front and back, clearly distinguishable in the revealing outfit.

Katelyn looked Jackie in the eye. "You're right," she said. "God does see your heart, but no one else will—especially the guys at youth service tonight." Katelyn was grieved for her friend and let out a sigh. "Jackie, we've been best friends since we played together in the nursery. You know I love you with all my heart."

"Yeah, *but* …" Jackie drawled out the word and sent a level gaze toward Katelyn. She had been listening to rules all her life and she wasn't planning on listening to her best friend spouting off. She was old enough to make her own decisions. Besides, she was feeling good about herself and having fun.

"But *nothing*," Katelyn said. She rose from her chair and squeezed Jackie's hand. "You know I love you, Jackie. Nobody knows better than I do what a really great person you are. I just wonder if you have considered how your new dressing choices are affecting your life."

"Affecting *my* life?"

"Yes, and others you care about."

Jackie lowered her hand from her hip and looked at her friend. She was still feeling defensive, but the sincerity in Katelyn's eyes softened her heart. "What do you mean?"

"Listen," Katelyn said, her voice low but firm. "We've grown up in church, and sometimes I think people expect us to absorb things and live certain standards without really understanding them."

"You've got that right."

"I know. But I also know there are people who are really concerned that we don't just follow rules, but we understand why God gave us guidelines—and the blessings that come into our lives when we choose to follow them."

"Blessings?"

"Yeah." Katelyn smiled at Jackie. "Blessings." Katelyn wrapped an arm around Jackie's shoulders and gave her a warm hug. "You said you only care about what God sees in your heart. Right?"

Jackie nodded. "I ... I really do."

"I know. I know you love God."

Jackie sniffed and leaned her head on Katelyn's shoulder. "Thanks for believing in me."

"I do believe in you, Jackie," Katelyn said. "I also believe what the Bible says about modesty is important. God gave us the Bible so we would know the best way to live."

"But see ... " Jackie sputtered and raised her head. "You're talking about the way we live again, and I just don't think it matters." Jackie freed herself from Katelyn's embrace, stomped to her bed and plopped down on it. "I'm wearing a skirt, for goodness sake. Isn't that enough? The Bible is about having a relationship with God, not what we wear or what we do."

Silence hung in the room before Katelyn spoke again. "Without a relationship with God, it *doesn't* matter what we wear or what we do."

Jackie sat quietly pondering the depth of Katelyn's words. A tiny light ignited in her spirit, and she turned to face her friend. "So it's not that God doesn't love me if I don't follow the rules ... but it's because I love God, I should live like the Bible says?"

"That's it. I think you've got it."

"OK. Maybe I do believe that how we live matters to God, but I think people can go overboard too. And it's totally confusing how some churches have one rule and another church has a different one. If we're all looking at the same Bible, shouldn't we all be reading and understanding the same thing? Have the same convictions?"

"I know what you mean," Katelyn said. "You know how I was telling you there were some people who really cared that we understand these things for ourselves?" Jackie nodded. "There is a new book that explains what the Bible says about modesty. Mom brought one home from ladies conference, and I think it would be great to go through it together."

"What if we still see things differently after we read it?"

"God doesn't expect us to be cookie-cutter Christians. There's room for personal style and personal convictions as long as they line up with the Bible and our choices are made with hearts to please God."

"I'd like to know for myself what the Bible really says."

"Me, too." Katelyn reached in her purse and pulled out a book. "Since I'm sleeping over tonight, maybe we can start looking at these things together."

Chapter One
Who Am I?

Who am I?

If you are like most girls, you have struggled with this question. Or how about this one? *Am I a person of worth?*

Imagine that right now you are sitting in a classroom full of girls. An attractively dressed middle-aged woman walks in the door and stands in front of the marker board until the buzzing in the room slows to silence. The woman's gaze moves from girl to girl, including you. When she has everyone's attention, she asks a question: "Do you consider yourself a person of worth?"

One girl, surrounded by a group of others, laughs and says, "Of course!" Another in the front row shrugs and mutters, "I guess so." Wrapping her arms around her middle, a girl in the back wonders in silence, while on the other side of the room another girl drops her head and closes her eyes. "I don't feel like one," she whispers.

What would be your answer?

If you belong to Jesus, you are part of the ultimate royal family. You have been adopted by the King who rules over every kingdom in Heaven and earth! When you were held hostage by sin with no hope of escape, Jesus paid a huge ransom for you. Why? Because He loves you very much.

No doubt you looked at the cover of this book. You know it is a book about modesty. No surprise there—so why start out with all the off-topic

Q&A? In order to really understand modesty as a biblical concept, we have to look past hemlines, habits, and even humility.

True modesty is centered in our relationship with God.

You are an adopted daughter of God, the King. That makes you a princess—not a little girl in a pink tutu playing dress up, but a mature, beautiful princess, the image of feminine elegance and refined manners. Perhaps you thought of the most popular princess of our time, Diana, Princess of Wales.

As far as words go, *princess* is a relatively new one. Not as new as *text message* or *lol*, but for centuries the daughter of royalty was not called *princess*, but *lady*. As God's lady, His princess, your value and identity are rooted in your relationship with Him. When you were born into God's royal family, regardless of your age, you became His child. From your first day until now, your value has been solidly, permanently established as a daughter of the King of all creation. "How great is the love the Father has lavished on us, that we should be called children of God" (I John 3:1, NIV).

Since we started with questions, here is one more. If we asked the same room full of girls we talked about earlier to rate their self-esteem on a scale from one to ten, we would hear (after some mumbling and groaning) numbers from sub-zero to ten-and-a-half. Depending on the time of the month or how her day is going, the same person might give a different answer in the afternoon than she gave over her morning bowl of Frosted Flakes. Think about this: If we measure our worth by how we are feeling, what others say about us, or what we imagine others think of us, we are using the wrong yardstick.

The first problem with rating self-esteem is that for a Christian, the concept itself is twisted. **Our esteem (our worth) is not in self at all. It is in God and His love for us.** If Jesus esteemed (valued, approved, or prized) our worth as the price He paid for us—brutal beatings, false accusations, betrayal, crucifixion, His own life—then we can know without a doubt we are of enormous value to God.

Not only are we of great value to God, Colossians 2:10 says we are complete in Him. Everyone has some type of flaw, some place we feel we don't measure up, with some more obvious than others. There will always be someone smarter, prettier, more talented, more popular, from a better background—and the list goes on. We must learn to be comfortable living in our own skin, and realize God made us the way He wanted us to be.

You were created in the image of our glorious God (Genesis 1:26). You and I carry God's likeness. We should feel great about ourselves. Right? Well, facts are facts, and we have to face them. Females, young and old, all come in different shapes, coloring, and sizes. We may not be happy with everything about our packaging, but the Bible says every one of us is fearfully and wonderfully made (Psalm 139:14). You may be a drop-dead knockout, plainer than a Plain Jane, or somewhere in between.

Regardless of how you look or even what you think about yourself, God thinks you are beautiful and desirable—so much so that He set up important safeguards for your protection, one of which is the subject of this book: modesty. Modesty is a precious gem given to God's people, His daughters, and His sons. Modesty will guard your virtue and moral character like a soldier standing watch at a palace door.

"Self-esteem had never been my strong point. I always wondered why I couldn't be beautiful and fair, and often times I became discouraged when I looked in the mirror. One day, while complaining about my pale skin, God asked me, 'Why do you criticize My creation?' Speechless, I stood in front of the mirror and began to cry. I had been doing it so long that I never considered I was complaining about the way God made me. But quickly God changed my heart.

"I began praying daily to see myself as God sees me, and I no longer allow the devil to tell me I am ugly. When I start to feel inadequate, I begin praising God for His marvelous works. There is no greater compliment I can receive than the Lord telling me I'm beautiful. Who cares if Neutrogena agrees? I am fearfully and wonderfully made!"

–Leah Gerth,
Memphis, Michigan

Moments of self-doubt are part of everyone's life. Everyone has areas in which they feel inadequate or that they just don't measure up. But when, through faith, we have a healthy God-esteem, we can walk with confidence.

God-esteem comes when we have a biblically-grounded way of looking at our value to God. It is a result of knowing what He has put into our lives and should not be confused with spiritual pride or vanity. God-esteem is an awareness that all our worth and abilities come from the One who made us. "Not that we are adequate in ourselves to consider anything as coming from ourselves, but our adequacy is from God" (II Corinthians 3:5, NASB).

One of the cool things about belonging to God is all the different "hats" we get to wear. I used to collect hats, and its funny how something as simple as putting on a hat can change the way you feel about yourself. Wearing different hats means filling different positions. Just to name a few, you are God's child, His friend, His servant, His fiancée, His ambassador, and His priest. Let's look at the "hat" of a priest. In I Peter 2:9 we learn, "But you are a chosen generation, a royal priesthood, a holy nation, His own special people, that you may proclaim the praises of Him who called you out of darkness into His marvelous light" (NKJV).

This verse tells us we are a distinct people. There is something that makes us stand out. We are separate, not common. The King James Version says we are "a peculiar people." I'm sure you've met some peculiar people in church (and out of church for that matter), but what peculiar means is that we are the purchased possession of God. **We are different for a reason.** The same verse tells us why: so we can declare the praises of God who called us out of darkness into His wonderful light.

A certain level of dignity is associated with membership in a royal priesthood. When I think of a royal priest serving God in the Holy of Holies, I don't think about some dude wearing a baseball cap and muscle shirt with a six-inch cross hanging from chains thick enough to haul a pick-up out of a ditch. One of the distinctions of godly Christian living, especially in times of ministering, is to keep the way we dress sacred or set apart for God.

Modesty comes from the Latin word *modestia*, which means *moderation*. Have you ever wondered if the people around you would consider you modest or moderate? Not given to excesses or self-indulgent? According to the Bible, they should. Philippians 4:5 says, "Let your moderation be known unto all men. The Lord is at hand." If we believe the Lord is near—"at hand"—we should choose to live in ways that invite a holy God into every part of our lives, even our closets. Our clothing choices should honor God and the sacrifice Jesus made for us on the cross. After all, what we wear advertises to whom we are committed—or wish to be associated.

This book is not about cramping your style. Instead, it's about giving you the tools you need to define your own style in harmony with the Word of God and your growing relationship with Him. **It's OK to follow after fashion if you follow it in modesty.** It feels nice to slip on the season's newest color or get a trendy purse. But keep in mind: We are in the world but not of it. God's people should have a "style all our own."

Casual days, formal occasions, church services, and everyday life—at every event and in every situation, our goal should be to dress decently and appropriately. The girl who chooses to honor God in modest dress and in the way she conducts herself chooses to be respected.

Several years ago a woman vacationed with her extended family. One of her in-laws told her that she believed this woman dressed modestly because she was overweight and ashamed of her body. It's true most overweight people would be happy to lose a few pounds, but the reason we live modestly, even on vacation, heavy or thin, is because we give God access to every part of our lives. All of our lives are set apart, sacred, because we live every moment in His presence.

Modesty is not a lack of being comfortable with our bodies. Female modesty is natural and God-given. We should regard our bodies as beautiful gifts from God—miracles of His creative work. God made the human body beautiful, but since the introduction of sin in the world, God instructed that human bodies should be covered. We will look more at what the Bible has to say about this in chapter 5.

In a letter to the editor published July 19, 2006, in the *News & Observer*, Claudia Barba of Garner, North Carolina, wrote: "Modest women know that our bodies are beautifully designed to be attractive to men. They are much too special for cheap, wholesale, public display. We reserve our bodies instead for the joyful, God-approved, exclusive sexual relationship of marriage.

"This choice has absolutely nothing to do with repression, insecurity or 'a skewed self-image.' Only a confident, strong woman is willing to dress to please God rather than her culture."

Go, Claudia! Great letter! This lady knows that the holiness and purity we practice in our physical bodies are directly related to the holiness and purity of an intimate marriage relationship. God created your beauty to satisfy the heart of a man—but *one* man, not every man. God made woman for man (I Corinthians 11:9), and your beauty is meant to be shared with your man, joyfully and freely—not to be lessened or cheapened by being put on public display.

In addition to our own integrity, God's girls should recognize the effect we have on others and help those who aren't our husbands keep their dignity by maintaining a pure thought life. Even if they are unaware of it, guys subconsciously read our body language. If we dress with dignity and carry ourselves with grace and femininity, guys are free to interact without unnecessary temptation and will more often treat us with respect and honor.

It's natural for girls to want to look pretty and attractive. There is certainly nothing wrong with that. The key to God-honoring modesty is keeping the right balance of desire for outward beauty and inward beauty and refraining from inappropriate excesses (I Timothy 2:9-10). Father John Hardon defined modesty in his *Catholic Dictionary* as "The virtue that moderates all the internal and external movements and appearance of a person."[1] Here's the bottom line: Modesty is moderation (self-control) in dress, conduct, attitude, and appearance. In simple terms, modesty is simplicity and decency. The opposite of modesty is vanity.

Modesty is not just about our dress. It is about the girl in the dress. God's girls are free to be beautiful, but not to be beguiling—attractive, but not tempting. Modesty protects girls from improper, inappropriate attention and says to the world, "I think I'm worth waiting for." That's something the one you marry and your Father will both appreciate.

Part of understanding what modesty is lies in understanding what it is not. Modesty is not wearing burlap bags for Jesus. Heaven forbid! The Bible says we are His ambassadors (II Corinthians 5:20), and we have a responsibility to represent His kingdom well—not crumpled and sloppy, or careless in our appearance. Revelation 16:15 says God's people are blessed when we watch and keep our garments.

As royalty in training, our official training manual, the Bible, tells us to "walk worthy of the vocation wherewith ye are called" (Ephesians 4:1). In ourselves we are unworthy, but now as part of the royal family of God, we should walk worthy of the office, or calling, God has so graciously given to us. We can achieve this, in part, by dressing in such a way that we are protected, respected, and have a clear conscience before God and others—not willfully provocative, tempting men with lustful thoughts or attracting the kind of attention that could lead us down dangerous paths.

> Baltasar Gracian, a Jesuit priest living in the 1600s, wrote: "Respect yourself if you would have others respect you." The truth is, people act differently according to what they wear, and people respond differently to us according to what we wear.

"I think a girl's self-esteem shows in how she dresses. People that feel lonely or depressed or are just struggling in their faith often seem to wear tighter dresses, lower shirts, shorter skirts, and the list goes on. But when we are happy with ourselves, where we are in God and in our lives, we tend to dress in ways Jesus would want us to."

–Rachel Riccardi,
Beaverton, Oregon

The daughter of Muhammad Ali, a famous boxer, shared her father's thoughts on modesty in her book, *More Than A Hero: Muhammad Ali's Life Lessons Through His Daughter's Eyes*. "'Hana, everything that God made valuable in the world is covered and hard to get to. Where do you find diamonds? Deep down in the ground, covered and protected. Where do you find pearls? Deep down at the bottom of the ocean, covered up and protected in a beautiful shell. Where do you find gold? Way down in the mine, covered over with layers and layers of rock. You've got to work hard to get to them.' He looked at me with serious eyes. 'Your body is sacred. You're far more precious than diamonds and pearls, and you should be covered too.'"[2]

Try This On...

Practicing modesty is exercising wisdom. When making clothing choices, we should take some things into consideration: What is what I am wearing saying about the condition of my heart? Whose approval am I seeking? Who am I advertising or associating with by the way I dress? Who defines beauty for me?

Who defines beauty for me?

Chapter Two

God's Design

| Why does God have rules anyway? | Why does He want Christians to live different in some ways than the rest of the world? After all, if God made the world, can it really be so bad? Parents, pastors, and Sunday school teachers talk about things like separation and holiness, but what harm is there in wanting to look like our friends and be a part of the fun they're having? To answer these questions, let's take a look at God's purpose and plan from the very beginning of creation.

Before time began, God formed a plan and then set it in motion. First He made the world and everything in it. Then He fashioned His ultimate masterpiece—the first man, Adam, made in His own image. (*Fashioned*—hmmm … sounds like God is into fashion. This could be good.) God knew what it felt like to be alone, so He gave Adam a specially designed helper and companion, his wife Eve.

Every evening God visited Adam and Eve in the Garden. They talked about their day, the things happening in the Garden, and just spent time together enjoying each other's company. Imagine what it must have been like to hang out and chill with God in the beauty and purity of the Garden of Eden. Hold onto that thought, because we're going to revisit it at the end of this chapter.

God made the earth and everything in it because He was looking for a relationship—one like He gave to Adam and Eve. Most girls can relate to that, hoping for a wonderful boyfriend who will some day be a wonderful husband. The desire for companionship every girl feels began first in the heart of God. He made us to be like Him, so those feelings are natural and good.

Adam and Eve, living the good life in a sinless, gorgeous paradise, disobeyed the only rule God gave them. They ate fruit from the tree in the middle of the Garden, the only thing God had refused them. To make things worse, after they disobeyed, they jilted God—stood up the Lord of lords for their evening walk. When God entered the Garden, Adam and Eve, wearing aprons of fig leaves over their private parts, hid themselves from God. They knew, even though they were wearing their new aprons, they were naked. The Hebrew word for *naked* in Genesis 3:7 means utterly naked and helpless. That's how Adam and Eve felt.

Did you know that you have a hidden treasure? You do. That's what Adam and Eve were trying to hide behind those fig leaves. The Persian word for paradise comes from the word *eden* which means enclosed garden. You have secret treasure that is meant to be hidden, enclosed, like a locked diary not to be opened for everyone to see.

|It's puzzling, isn't it?| Adam and Eve were naked all along but they weren't ashamed. How could that be? When God made Adam, He made him in His image. Psalm 104:2 tells us God is clothed in light, and Adam, made in the glorious image and perfect sinless nature of God, had the same appearance as God. He was covered in light. That's why he and Eve (made in the image of Adam, I Corinthians 11:7), could be naked and unashamed in God's presence. Before their disobedience, **Adam and Eve were clothed—clothed in the light of God's glory and purity.**

It's like this: If you have a light bulb turned on, you don't really see the light bulb. You see the light radiating out of it. When the light is turned off, you see the bare bulb. The glory, the light that covered Adam and Eve, faded when they disobeyed God's instructions. As the glory faded, their eyes were opened. They knew they were naked, and they were ashamed.

God knows the end from the beginning. He knew everything He set in motion was going to fall, but He had a plan in place. God knew what Adam and Eve had done, but in His great love, He called for them to come to Him. Frightened and ashamed, they came out from their hiding places. They talked about what they had done and God responded to their sin by covering their nakedness with tunics made from an animal skin. As a result of their disobedience, Adam and Eve lost their own innocence, and the first innocent life was killed to pay for their wrongs and cover their shame. We'll look at this in-depth in chapter 5.

Before they sinned Adam and Eve walked in purity, but after sin they struggled. Their human natures resisted God's voice and fought against their own deep desires for relationship with God. But remember, God knew all this was going to happen. He was prepared. He made a way for men and women to have a relationship with Him after Adam and Eve's disobedience. But now blood and the death of the innocent became a part of that relationship. Starting in the Garden of Eden, passing through time and millions of sacrifices, finally Calvary's cross became the ultimate sacrifice followed by the ultimate victory, Jesus' resurrection in a garden tomb.

The Bible says God is holy, and to have a relationship with Him, we are commanded to be holy too. Not "holier than thou," but holy like He is. Holiness, or being separated, isn't just an outside thing. When our inside is full of Light, and when we understand God's nature and plan for our lives, the work that starts on the inside shows up on the outside in our attitudes, the way we conduct ourselves, and the clothes we wear.

The Bible says God is holy, and to have a relationship with Him, we are commanded to be holy too.

"Growing up in a small town in Iowa, people tend to know just who you are. We are twins, Soph and Vanny George, and we're not ashamed of our modesty or holiness. While attending school we were not embarrassed about our attire or standards, choosing instead to be proud of who we are and how we presented ourselves. Along with a friend, at our school we were known as The Skirt Girls.

"After years of being consistent in our dress and faithful to church and our beliefs, we'd earned the name Skirt Girls or The Skirts (depending on the person) from a few rowdy boys. The boys, trying to get a reaction out of us, called us The Skirts often, hoping we'd get upset or mad about it. When we weren't fazed by it, it became common among our peers, eventually replacing our names. Going down the hall, instead of a 'Hi, girls,' we'd get a 'What's up, skirts?' and what started out as an attempt to tease quickly turned into a positive.

"Each year, as most schools do, we have spirit week. Every day would be something new: Mismatch Day, Inside-Out Day, Superhero Day. One particular year, we had Twin Day. For this event, the girls who dressed modestly got together and decided to make matching shirts for Twin Day that said, "The Skirts" on them. We wore them and they were a hit! Just because you don't dress the way the rest of your school looks doesn't mean that you're not cool. We had many friends and Soph was even voted homecoming queen, all without compromising."

–Savannah and Sophia George,
Anamosa, Iowa

Imagine you are engaged to Mr. Hunk-o-holy-mania. You want to please him. If he likes blue, you put blue on your shopping list. If he likes Wendy's, you suddenly start craving Jr. Bacon Cheeseburgers and Frostys. If he's into sports, you ask your brother for enough info to understand what he's talking about. If he doesn't like macaroni and cheese, you won't fix it, even if it's been your favorite since you were two years old. Why? Because you love him! Should a Christian girl be any less concerned about pleasing the Lord?

In the Old Testament, before the Temple was built and Jesus made a way for us to have direct access to God, men interacted with God in the Tabernacle. The Tabernacle, a tent-like structure, was set up in the middle of the camp, apart from all that was common or sinful around it. A person could only approach this holy meeting place according to God's plan. Like little tabernacles placed in the middle of the world around us, God sets us apart from all that's sinful in the world. He wants us to know Him and show the world how to approach Him—in salvation, in praise, and in worship. Our heart becomes His home, a holy place where His Spirit dwells. Not just God with us, but God in us, forever and ever, amen!

This chapter is about God's purpose and plan for our lives and how that relates to modesty. We've laid the foundation and now let's look at some of the reasons for clothes according to the Bible.

- Clothes were given by God to cover our physical bodies (Genesis 3:21).
- Clothes separate the girls from the boys (Deuteronomy 22:5).
- Following after the Spirit, even in dressing choices, helps us avoid sin (Galatians 6:7-8).
- Dressing modestly shows the world who God's people are (Romans 12:2).
- Proper clothing appropriately covers God's temple—our bodies (I Corinthians 6:19).
- We honor God in the way we present our bodies (I Corinthians 6:20).
- Our clothing should reflect biblical concepts of what's decent and what's modest (I Timothy 2:9).
- Our dress should complement, not take away from, our walk with God (I Peter 3:3-5).
- Our clothes should not identify us with ungodly activities/people or be worn to manipulate others (Proverbs 7:10).

Some say, "You can't judge a book by its cover," but when it comes to clothing and modesty issues, the cover tells so much about what's really inside. Our clothes make many different statements, including where we are spiritually. Statements on a gothic website[1] showed that a high percentage of gothic dressers wear black because black is how they feel inside. They also said it makes them feel protected, and (of course) it is slimming (every girl knows that). The gothic subgroup of our society is not one group in itself. It also includes punk rockers and all their various subcategories: standard, hard core, skate punk, pop punk, crust punk, droog, and suicidals. Punkers have to know not only that they are punk, but also which subcategory they are dressing to identify with.

Gangs have their own colors, and they are very important to them. Innocent people have lost their lives when they walked into gang territory wearing the wrong colors. Then there's the prep look, the bohemian, and the list goes on.

|What about labels?| Have you considered we actually pay to advertise for businesses when we buy and wear their labels on our clothes? It's true—from a little seagull flying above our hearts to company names splashed across our t-shirts. I'm not saying we should only choose clothes that don't have visible labels, but think about the image you project when you wear a label. The designers know they are selling more than clothes. Ralph Lauren said, "I don't design clothes, I design dreams." Calvin Klein boasts, "I'm a sexual person, and that's reflected in my clothes and my advertisements." **The image a designer is projecting is the image you associate with when you wear his clothes and accessories.**

Murdered Italian designer Gianni Versace said, "You decide what you are, what you want to express, by the way you dress and the way you live." The fashion industry knows the real deal on why we wear what we wear. They make their living at it. Big designers are actually referred to as "houses"—for example, "the House of Versace" or "the House of Chanel." Isn't that interesting? I hope my dressing choices say, "The House of Jesus." The Bible tells us that when we are baptized, we "put on" Christ (Galatians 3:27). We're wearing His name.

The Bible also tells older women like me (not old, but older) to teach the younger women. In Titus 2:4-5, Paul told me through his letter to teach you a few things. That's a request worthy of breaking out the *Strong's Concordance*. There are several things he mentioned, some that have to do with marriage. We won't cover them all, but the first thing he said was to be sober. That doesn't mean the opposite of being drunk. What it means is being moderate, sensible, and responsible. That goes along with another point he mentioned: being discreet, or having a logical, reasoned mind and being self-controlled. We are called to be chaste, a word that means modest and pure from worldliness.

Why are older women supposed to teach these things to the younger ones? The end of verse five tells us, "so that no one will malign the Word of God." To malign means to speak harmful untruths. In other words, we are not to give in to culture, seeking after whatever pleases us for the moment, but we should take a stand for purity and be a role model so people won't have bad things to say against God's church.

In the New Testament, purity and holiness are often used interchangeably. Jesus taught that impure thoughts lead to impure actions (Matthew 15:19). Moral purity begins with a mind devoted to God and should result in the modest life Paul was talking about in his letter to Titus.

"A friend and I were browsing a very busy store one day and the owner was helping us search for a particular item. Once we were in an area away from other customers, he turned and said, 'I know that you are holy ladies, and I need you to pray for me.' With that he began to tell us some of his struggles. What amazed me with this conversation is that he did not say, 'I think you are Christians.' He used the term 'holy.' Something set us apart that day from the other customers roaming his store, something that drew him to us and allowed him to share his need."

– Mary Loudermilk,
Florissant, Missouri

So what is modesty? Are you scanning this book looking for the official "Bible Dressing Code" so you can make sure you are measuring up? If you flip to other chapters you will see some tips and teaching, but not a checklist. **Modesty comes from a godly heart, not a checklist.** Having a clearly defined set of rules is the easy way out. In some ways checklists may be helpful, but in another way, they can encourage people to look for the bottom line—the bare minimum necessary to measure up to what's expected or considered acceptable.

Looking for the bottom-line requirement is not pursuing excellence, something every Christian should strive for. Instead of asking for the minimum (what we can get away with), we should seek to please God and live in ways that bring Him glory. If we're living by a checklist, we'll find ways around the rules. Any lines drawn will be pushed further and further until the original line is completely unrecognizable. It will happen, one small step at a time, as our inborn sense of modesty, our natural reaction to shame, is desensitized and ultimately ignored.

God created clothing to cover Adam and Eve's shame, the shame that came from their sin. The clothing God provided had a purpose—to cover mankind's sinful nature and the shame of breaking God's sacred authority. Modesty is a secondary issue that reveals the most important one—the condition of our hearts. Modesty is at the center of our relationship with God—an acknowledgement of our sinful human nature and our need for covering.

This isn't calculus, girls. It actually makes sense when we look at the big picture. In addition to honoring God and having a right concept of sin and covering, modesty is a blessing and protection in our lives. **Modesty attracts righteousness. Immodesty attracts immorality.** "Do not be deceived, God is not mocked; for whatever a man sows, that he will also reap. For he who sows to his flesh will of the flesh reap corruption, but he who sows to the Spirit will of the Spirit reap everlasting life" (Galatians 6:7-8, NKJV).

God made men to want to look at women, and there's something in women that wants to be looked at. My personal philosophy is that men look because they have a natural instinct to find, based on a girl's appearance of health, strength, and beauty, the one who would make the best mate and mother for their children. Women want to be looked at because they want to be chosen, to be worthy of gaining a man's love and security and then keeping it. Just remember, although these tendencies are basic human nature, in public interactions, men and women should be covered and appropriate. Private intimate relations are between one man and one woman in that enclosed garden paradise we talked about before. Modesty protects that relationship.

In his book, *Christian Modesty and the Public Undressing of America*, Baptist pastor Jeff Pollard wrote, "Being drawn to a person's God-given beauty is one thing; having one's eyes directed to another's body by a sensually designed garment is another **… any apparel designed to draw the eye to the erotic zones of the body cannot fill the requirement for biblical decency.**"[2] He goes on to make some other great points: "Scriptural evidence convinced me that modern swimwear is immodest nakedness; and historical evidence convinced me it was designed to be so. … Christian morality simply caved in. … The cry of Feminists is 'It's my body, and I'll do what I want.' The cry of the modern Evangelical is 'It's my liberty, and I'll do what I want.' Nevertheless, the declaration of the Scripture is this: 'What, know ye not that your body is the temple of the Holy Ghost which is in you … and ye are not your own?'"

The world may set the fashion trends people follow after, but Christians should set the example and follow after God (Ephesians 5:1). Modesty is a lost friend in a world where people live for pleasure, and even mothers worship at the altar of fashion, neglecting to teach their children to live moral lives. Yes—moral lives. Putting on the clothes we wear in public is just as much a moral act as taking them off in public is an immoral one.

I told you we were going to revisit the issue of hanging out with God in a pure, sinless environment. So here we go. I recently read the third chapter of Philippians and was amazed when I came to the last verse that said we, God's people, will be fashioned (once again, God is *fashioning* people) "like unto His glorious body." His glorious body is the body of Jesus, the image of the invisible God. Let's think about this now. God is a glorious God of light. He made Adam and Eve in His image, clothed in glory. Their sin and disobedience stripped their glorious covering from them and God graciously gave them physical coverings (through a blood sacrifice) to hide their shame.

Throughout all time, God has revealed Himself as glorious light (Exodus 25:17-22). Jesus entered the world to save us, to cover us and our sin once and for all with His blood sacrifice. He was God, but He did not come in His glory; He came in flesh—God without the glory. He lived humbly among the people He created and taught them about the concepts behind the dos and don'ts in the Bible. Not just rules, but the reasons for the rules—our relationships with God and others. The disciples got a sneak preview of Jesus' glorified body before His resurrection (Matthew 17:2). His face looked like the sun and His clothes like light. After He died and rose from the grave, Jesus walked through walls and appeared out of nowhere in His resurrected, glorified body.

> There's a churchy word called *glorification* that describes this entire process—this renewal of creation. What it all boils down to is this: God created men glorious and without sin. Men sinned and lost their glory. Jesus came without glory to make a way for men to have a relationship with God. After the resurrection Jesus received a glorified body, and we will too if we are in Him (Philippians 3:9). We will be like Jesus both physically and morally (without sin). So everything will be the way God intended in the first place. God and man, together, having one pure and glorious relationship forever.

|This excites me! What about you?| Of course, we live our days in these earthly bodies, but for now, God clothes us with the garments of salvation (Isaiah 61:10). And just as surely as we have worn flesh in this world, we will be like Him in the next (Romans 8:30; I Corinthians 15:49).

Try This On...

Our life here is preparing us to be like Jesus, and it is God's purpose and plan for our lives from before time began. He calls us to be like Him, and that is why we give ourselves to living a holy life in the here and now—living, learning, and loving God.

He calls us to be like Him.

Chapter Three
Falling in Love

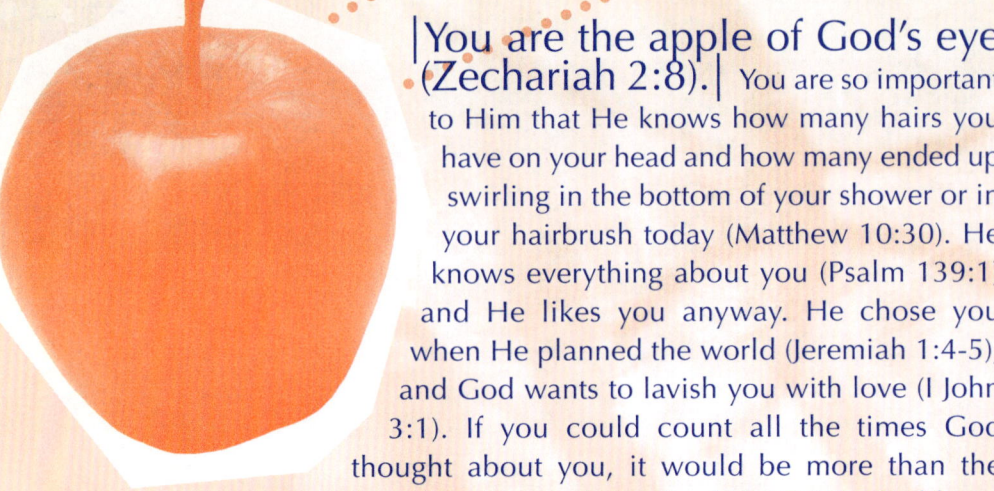

|You are the apple of God's eye (Zechariah 2:8).| You are so important to Him that He knows how many hairs you have on your head and how many ended up swirling in the bottom of your shower or in your hairbrush today (Matthew 10:30). He knows everything about you (Psalm 139:1) and He likes you anyway. He chose you when He planned the world (Jeremiah 1:4-5), and God wants to lavish you with love (I John 3:1). If you could count all the times God thought about you, it would be more than the grains of sand on the earth (Psalm 139:17-18). God loves you with an everlasting, unending love (Jeremiah 31:3) and you are His treasure (Exodus 19:5).

When I became a born-again Christian, everything in me longed to give myself completely to Him. I was young, full of excitement and fun, but I had never felt love like Jesus downloaded into my heart. I was sold out! So many things began to change, beginning with my priorities. My first concern was not to win souls or have revivals; I just wanted to be with Jesus—in church, in fellowship with other Christians, and most of all in our special time together the first thing every morning and before going to bed each night.

If you weren't raised in church, you know exactly what I'm talking about—the thrill of finding true joy and happiness in Jesus. Or maybe you grew up on the pew. You lisped through "Deep and Wide" in toddler class, were baptized in the beginner class, learned the books of the Bible in junior class, and on up the line. No matter when or how we come to know Him, once we understand His tremendous love for us, something deep inside longs to return His love more than anything else.

The great philosopher Dr. Seuss describes love like this: "You know you're in love when you can't fall asleep because reality is finally better than your dreams." God's love is more than a dream, although it does seem unreal! Just think about it. There is nothing you or I could have ever done or given to earn the love of the holy God of the universe. Jesus did it all and then freely offered all to us. No wonder people write songs about God's amazing grace and amazing love.

If we are not careful, we can forget the incredible love we felt when we first met Jesus—take Him for granted, treat His holiness lightly, and let our love dwindle (Revelation 2:4). Wouldn't it be terrible if one day God looked at you and said, "I can tell you don't love Me anymore by the way you have been acting"? God deserves our best.

"Having therefore these promises, dearly beloved, let us cleanse ourselves from all filthiness of the flesh and spirit, perfecting holiness in the fear of God" (II Corinthians 7:1). When we are tempted to put things or our emotions before our relationship with God, when thoughts and feelings are whirling like a tornado on the prairie, it's wise to take a step back and consider the final outcome giving in would bring. If the result is something God calls sin, put a stop to what you are doing immediately—and never go back to it. Love doesn't look back. Love looks ahead.

Speaking of love, wouldn't it be exciting to get a love letter? Sure! We all have, even if we haven't thought of it this way. We have a wonder of a love letter written from God to us—the Bible. God should be listed in the *Guinness Book of World Records* for the longest love letter ever. It begins in Genesis and ends in Revelation with 66 books, 1,189 chapters, 31,173 verses, 593,493 words. And just in case you were wondering, the very heart of the Bible, the verse at the very center, is Psalm 118:8: "It is better to trust in the LORD than to put confidence in man."

God's Word, His personal love letter to you and me, helps us understand how He thinks and feels about us. The Bible tells us in I Samuel 16:7 that God looks at our hearts. It also says men look on the outward appearance. These words weren't written so we could have an excuse for being careless about how we look (since God looks at our hearts). They were not written to make us feel bad for looking at the "outer" person. This verse was given to help us understand some important facts. Looking on the outward is just the natural way a human mind works, not good or bad. Appearances do count, and we should live a lifestyle, in our actions and in our dress, that reflects our commitment to God.

If we love God, our hearts and our dress will honor Him.

Modesty is an important topic to study, but realize it is only a side issue. Before we turn our focus to an in-depth look at biblical modesty, I hope to inspire you to seek God with your whole heart. When you do, modesty will be part of the result. If we love God, our hearts and our dress will honor Him.

"The topic of modesty goes beyond the length of our skirts and height of our necklines. It goes straight into our hearts. Why do we do what we do? Did God put boundaries in His Word to give people a reason to ridicule us or ruin our social lives? No. He gave them to protect us.

"God desires to reveal to you how precious and beautiful you are. He formed you and chose your structure, your eyes, your own unique personality and talents. He took His time to create you in His image.

"After years of trying to find myself by altering my appearance, I finally found God. Now anything I can do to get closer to God I need to do regardless of the price I have to pay. He paid the ultimate price and now I aspire to give Him my all.

"Our peers may not understand the importance of modesty in our lives, but God wants our minds, hearts, and bodies to be pure and set apart because He is pure and holy. This isn't mission impossible, but it does take work to submit ourselves and our bodies to God in our sin-saturated world. When it comes right down to it, we will choose to serve either our flesh or our God. But there is hope. God said He would help us and guide us. He convicts our hearts when we do something wrong so we can repent and make things right with Him.

"The enemy of our souls wants us to believe we are not good enough to go into this world looking like godly Christian young ladies. I have found it to be an honor and privilege to dress according to the Word of God. I have learned the way of God is the best way, and a way anyone can choose to take."

–Angela Harwood, Elliot Lake, Ontario

When we stop and think about how much love God has shown us, how could we purposely choose to offend Him? Or question Him? What person could think they know better than God—or that God might be wrong? **Asking sincere questions is a good thing,** and answering real questions is the purpose of this book. Hopefully we all want to understand God's Word (II Timothy 2:15). Asking questions so you can understand something is not the same thing as arrogantly questioning whether the Bible is truer than our thoughts or if we should even bother obeying its teachings. This type of questioning opens the door to doubt and human rationalizing and often leads down a path of faulty excuses for selfish choices.

Proverbs 3:7 tells us we should not be wise in our own eyes. Our human natures can tempt us to place too much value on our own opinions, making them higher in our minds than God's Word. This kind of upside-down thinking feeds the monsters of pride and self-importance that each of us carries—monsters that need to be starved instead of fed. It's not our decision to decide what's "good enough for me," but to honor God in our bodies (I Corinthians 6:20) and pursue the path of holiness laid out in the Word.

Arguments that God wants His people to live *free* from any boundaries or restrictions are arguments based on pride and wrong thinking. As David K. Bernard wrote in *Essentials of Holiness*, "True holiness is not 'freedom' to act and look like the world … but freedom from the need to conform to the world."[1]

Take a moment to ask yourself this question: "Am I faithful to what God says, or do I try to compromise His words with thoughts that never came from Him?" We must never allow anyone or anything, including ourselves, to take our focus off what's most important—our relationship with God.

The offer of a New Testament love relationship with God requires more than Old Testament laws ever did—and there were a lot of laws in the Old Testament. Aren't you glad we don't have to follow all the restrictions Moses gave to the Jewish people in the books of the Law? Although we aren't required to live according to all the old ceremonial laws, serving God still requires effort on our part. It's not something we do once and we're done—like losing our baby teeth or something. **Total commitment is a one-time pledge followed by a lifetime of choosing** to continue that commitment.

Have you ever stopped to think about God's holiness? Or wonder since He is holy, is He comfortable living in me? Are unrepentant, unholy actions and attitudes part of my everyday life that make the Holy Ghost feel like moving out and moving on—or at least taking a vacation in a friendlier environment? I have good news. God is not looking for excuses to dump us like yesterday's coffee grounds. He's invested too much in us for that, but He does want our relationships to be mutual, give-and-take on both sides.

"I just love that new perfume!" "Don't you love that new music project?" "Love ya, bff." "I love you, Daddy." "I love you so much, darling." "I love You, Jesus, with everything in me." All these expressions of love make the point that there are different kinds and levels of love—even an order of importance. A Christian might think putting God at the top of their love list is the right way of thinking, but a better way is putting Jesus at the center and letting everything else radiate around that core relationship with God. It's a whole different way of thinking—not just "I love God best and have all these less important things underneath," but "My love for God is the core of who I am, and it affects everything else in my life." God's love flows through every level of our existence.

Do you remember Jesus' answer to the question, which is the greatest commandment?

"Jesus said to him, 'You shall love the Lord your God with all your heart, with all your soul, and with all your mind.' This is the first and great commandment. And the second is like it: 'You shall love your neighbor as yourself'" (Matthew 22:37-39, NKJV). Jesus said that every rule and prophecy hang on these two commandments (commandments, not suggestions, by the way.) Even biblical guidelines for modesty? Yes!

The greatest commandment deals with our love for God. Because of God's love for us, we belong to Him. We are His ambassadors to the world. When we dress modestly, we honor Him and represent Him well. Modesty doesn't seek its own attention but points people to Jesus.

The second commandment has to do with our relationship with others. If we love others, we care about how our lives affect them. Dressing modestly shows love for the women around us by maintaining a spirit of humility, not feeding pride, or being part of some competition where everyone loses.

For the guys around us, dressing modestly helps them maintain pure thoughts, not tempting them to lustful thinking. That's a form of defrauding (promising something you can't deliver) mentioned in I Thessalonians 4:3-7. The King James version uses the word "defraud," but let's look at this in the NIV for a plainer understanding: "It is God's will that you should be sanctified: that you should avoid sexual immorality; that each of you should learn to control his own body in a way that is holy and honorable, not in passionate lust like the heathen, who do not know God; and that in this matter no one should wrong [defraud] his brother or take advantage of him. The Lord will punish men for all such sins, as we have already told you and warned you. For God did not call us to be impure, but to live a holy life."

People sometimes confuse innocence and purity. We receive innocence from sin as a gift of God, but purity is what we give back to Him when we seek to live according to God's Word and the leading of His Spirit. When we come in contact with people who live differently than the Bible says, we may find ourselves influenced in less than good or pure ways. Maintaining a close relationship with God sometimes means refusing to think about or participate in certain things. Remember, our conscience and the Word guide us. Obey with joy, and God's pure love for you will boomerang back to Him. God's pure love for us helps us love Him purely in return—to purely love Him, His Word, those in authority over us, our Christian brothers and sisters, and the lost world.

One last point on the second great commandment, how modesty shows love for others. Modesty sets us apart from sinful lifestyles. People notice when we dress modestly. If our words and actions match up, this will be a powerful witness to the unsaved. Do we love those who don't know Jesus enough to be different? Jesus came to give us life. When we invite Him into our lives, He lives out His life through ours. Let me tell you, we get the bargain in that deal. We give God our sins and problems, worries, doubts, and pains. We get the God of glory, peace, grace, and truth sharing in our lives, directing our footsteps, and blessing us in ways we never dreamed.

As Christians, we represent God's hands and feet to the world—our whole body really. We need to remember that

> Do we love those who don't know Jesus enough to be different?

when we are dressing ourselves, we are dressing physical representations of Jesus to the world. The way we dress has the potential to either confirm or undermine our Christian faith in the eyes of those around us. Our style of dress is one powerful way we choose to *reflect* Jesus or *reject* Jesus.

The Bible tells us to set an example of good *in everything* so people won't have anything bad to say about our lives (Titus 2:7-8). Of course this applies to more than modesty, but modesty in clothing and actions can speak louder and clearer of our faith than thousands of words we might say or even verses we can quote.

|Our bodies are the temple of the Holy Spirit.|

God lives inside us and He cares about the way we take care of His home. In the beginning God invites us to come to Him. He takes us as we are, but once we are born into the family, He wants us to grow. He didn't give us spiritual life so we could play happily on a heavenly nursery floor until the Rapture—depending on others to take care of our needs and our messes.

As we grow, we learn the Word and follow its teachings. In my experience, with one small change at a time, things in my natural life began lining up with my new spiritual life. God is a great teacher, down to the smallest detail. I learned that when His Spirit made me question something, I should respond right away by stopping whatever I was doing or getting rid of things that displeased Him—not because I was told *the rules*, but in response to His love.

It's our responsibility to keep our spirits in agreement with His. One way we accomplish this is by reading the Bible and asking questions to trusted people like our pastors and Sunday school teachers. Make sure once you get in the race, you stay on the right track—growing in your walk with God, never taking a step back. When I was first saved, one piece of advice from my pastor really helped me as I learned to walk with God and hear His voice: "If you need to ask if something is right or wrong," he said, "then you can be sure the Lord is dealing with you to *not* do that."

Sometimes spiritual things seem hard. We are told to let God speak to us, but then we question, "How do I know when it's God speaking to me?" God doesn't want communication with Him to be hard. It's easier than we think—even easier than texting a friend. God is as close as the mention of His name, and His batteries never lose their charge. He loves it when we talk to Him, and He never drops our call. God wants us to learn to listen for His voice. **He speaks to us through our conscience and through His Word.** It's that simple.

As we already discussed, the Bible is God's love letter. Throughout all time, God sent messages to those He loves. In today's world, people have lots of crazy ways they show love. The rage from Hollywood to high schools is to display your love by getting *inked* or tattooed. Lovers get matching tattoos, only to have them removed and tattooed over a year down the road when that relationship has fizzled and their flame is now burning for someone else.

God has taken more than ink for you. He has written your name on His hand. "See, I have inscribed you on the palms of My hands" (Isaiah 49:16a, NKJV). More than ink-filled needles poked Jesus' flesh on our behalf. He was beaten beyond recognition and nails were pounded in His wrists and feet as He hung on the cross and took on my sin and your sin. His love poured out for you and me. God loves with true passion—a word with a two-fold meaning: love and suffering. The cross tells the story of true, passionate love, a love that requires sacrifice.

Because of His passionate love for us, God always longs to restore broken relationships. We can read one example of this in the Bible. A woman caught in sin was dragged before Jesus for judgment. She deserved capital punishment, the death sentence, but Jesus did not accuse her. He knelt and wrote in the dirt or sand until all her accusers realized their own sin and unworthiness to condemn the woman. When all others had slipped away, the woman remained alone with the only One worthy to judge her. But instead of judgment, she received a message from Jesus that changed her life.

We don't know what Jesus wrote as the woman trembled on the ground near His feet, but I like to think of it as a love letter written in the sand. We all fall short from time to time in our walk with God, but God doesn't want to condemn us. He loves us. Today He offers the same message He spoke to the woman caught in sin: "Neither do I condemn you ... go and sin no more."

Modesty is just the tip of the iceberg—the small part that peaks above the waterline with so much more still beneath the surface. Unseen things are more important than the seen. They can sink unsinkable ships. Think about this. What good would it do to drive a loaded Corvette if the brakes didn't work? The ride might be fun for a few minutes, but it would end in disaster. But when the car looks great and all the parts are working—oh, yeah, let it roll!

Try This On...

The way we conduct ourselves, in manner and apparel, are not simply acts of obedience to a holy God—although that would be reason enough to observe them—but they are acts of love. God is madly, passionately in love with us! How will we respond?

God is madly, passionately in love with us!

Chapter Four
Inside Out

|Have you ever wondered| why if we're all serving the same God, how come standards are different from church to church, even in churches of the same denomination? And what is a standard anyway? That doesn't even sound like a nice word.

LOVE

A standard is defined as an average or normal requirement or a requirement of moral conduct. One definition that really got my attention was a flag or a banner. That reminded me of a Sunday school song, "His Banner over Me Is Love." **Modesty is a banner of love.**

I think a lot of people get hung up on a phrase some teachers and ministers use: *holiness standards*. We can't be holy apart from God. Holiness comes only through God's gift of grace, but how we respond to the gift of His holiness—out of love, reverence, and thankfulness—that's the key.

We respond to Jesus by obeying His commands. Not just Acts 2:38 (hey, we all know that one, right?), but also His greatest commandments—first to love God and then to love others as we love ourselves. If we truly love others, we won't be stumbling blocks in their path as they try to please God in the area of sexual purity.

If we truly love God, we will try our best to represent Him well. The Bible says we are living letters from Him to the world, His ambassadors, His representatives. We honor Him and the responsibilities He has given us by the way we conduct ourselves and dress. We aren't supposed to "keep up with the Joneses" or Madison Avenue, but we are free to live in the peace that comes when we stay in the boundaries of God's Word.

If we have a Christ-like spirit of meekness, we won't want to wear sexy or even flashy clothing and accessories that attract attention to ourselves (or our body parts). Instead, we will choose to wear humility, grace, and dignity. Eccentric singer and songwriter Cyndi Lauper said, "Somebody did … tell me that my clothes were so loud they couldn't hear me sing." What are your clothes saying? Are they drowning out the message of your salvation song?

And how about wearing a smile? We have so much to be thankful for. We shouldn't walk around looking like we were baptized in sour pickle juice! If we have the joy of the Lord on the inside, we should wear it on the outside. A smile is powerful. Dale Carnegie, the author of *How to Win Friends and Influence People,* said, "The expression a woman wears on her face is far more important than the clothes she wears on her back."

If we have righteousness on the inside, we should wear that on the outside. If we have holiness on the inside, we should also wear it on the outside. If we have corruption on the inside, it will be noticed on the outside.

If we have a sensual spirit on the inside, it will show up on the outside. Yikes! "As a man thinks in his heart, so is he" (Proverbs 23:7).

One verse often quoted on the importance of holy living is Hebrews 12:14 which says that without holiness, no one will see the Lord. These are strong words and not to be taken lightly. I agree with them, but I also wonder if we may have unintentionally only focused on the last part of this verse. The complete sentence reads, "Follow peace with all men, and holiness, without which no man shall see the Lord." The Bible says follow peace *and* holiness. If we are contentious and judge others, that doesn't cut it. If my convictions are tighter than others', it's not my place to correct or judge. If they are looser, I should still live according to Bible teachings and keep my pastor's guidelines. Think of our pastor as our coach, and we are on his team. Let's suit up and get in the game. What we're wearing should clearly show we are on God's team.

God calls our bodies "tabernacles"—or "tents" (II Corinthians 5:1). In the Old Testament people worshiped in the Tabernacle, which was built according to the very detailed instructions God gave Moses. All the lovely things used in making the Tabernacle were not displayed on the outside. The gold and precious gems were on the inside.

As we continue to look at modesty, I think it's wise to ask ourselves if our focus has been more on outward beauty than inward. Do we spend as much time beautifying the inside as we do dressing up the outside?

Let's take a look at standards. There are basically three categories:

1) Unchanging biblical principles.
These go beyond time and culture (such as sexual purity and separation from the world).

2) Local church guidelines.
These are teamwork principles of dress and conduct for unity in the local church. The Bible gives clear lines on some issues, but other lines are not always easily defined. Picture it like this: If sin is a mountain, just where does the mountain stop and start? In local churches, pastors set these guidelines for their congregations.

3) Personal convictions.
These are strong beliefs we are personally convinced of, values that may be stricter than local church guidelines. Convictions are individual and personal, but this is the bottom line—every standard should line up with the unchanging principles in the Word of God.

In chapter 3, we talked about following the great commandment to love God and the second commandment to love others as ourselves. Thinking about this, let's take a deeper look at how the way we dress affects others.

If we love God and our brothers, we won't be careless in our dressing choices, but careful. God made men and women different. Generally, women respond to physical touch while men respond to the things they see. It just makes sense that if it is wrong for a young man to touch a young woman for a sensual response, it is wrong for her to dress in a way that will cause a sensual response in the young men looking at her.

Anne Richardson, a mentor in Saint John, New Brunswick, asks some good questions to help her students evaluate their decisions. "Who reigns on the throne of your heart? Is it you—or is it God?" She follows up with a serious thought: "You will never be able to run from evil until you have fully surrendered to God. When He becomes your first love, keeping yourself pure will be your number one priority, and much easier to do."

Think about the way people dress in church these days, or even church camp. It's easy to spot girls who follow guidelines about appropriate necklines, lengths for hems, and so on, yet have lost the concept of modesty. They wear clothes that look shrink-wrapped to their bodies, revealing every curve and shape—like a hand in a glove.

If we just follow rules, our human nature will come up with ways to get around them. But when we have a relationship with God, He loves us enough to make us uncomfortable when we are about to do something wrong. If we put on something immodest, He will give us a check—a little tug in our hearts—but it's up to us which voice we will follow. Our dressing choices are truly *our* dressing choices.

Here are some definitions of modesty from Noah Webster's original *American Dictionary of the English Language* published in 1828.[1]

- Properly restrained by a sense of propriety
- Not forward or bold
- Not presumptuous or arrogant not boastful
- Moderate
- Not excessive or extreme
- Retiring and unobtrusive manners
- Modesty results from purity of mind
- Unaffected modesty is the sweetest charm of female excellence, the richest gem in the diadem of their honor.

Modesty is more about what comes from a pure mind than what we wear. While this is true, it is also true that our outward appearance is a direct reflection of our hearts and minds. Modesty and holiness are two different concepts, but according to Wendy Shalit, Jewish author of *A Return to Modesty,* **"Modesty is intertwined with holiness**—in the presence of the holy, one must cover up."[2] And the concept of modesty goes beyond what we put on our bodies. There is a modest walk and there is a swagger. There is a haughty look and an attitude of being humble. We choose the things we wear and the way we carry ourselves, and all should line up with the biblical teaching of modesty.

Bible-based standards, sometimes made fun of or considered old fashioned, are not wrong in themselves. The word *standard* is used in the Bible twenty-two times. Biblical guidelines are not legalism (a word never used in the Bible). "Legalism" means putting too much importance on rules in a way that can lead to shallow thinking and a lack of consideration of God's grace and mercy.

|Every relationship comes with boundaries.| Throughout the Bible we read about prophets preaching against sin and giving warnings to people about the consequences of sin. Think about Jonah and Jeremiah. These guys had some tough words to deliver, but God called them to do it, even if their messages weren't popular.

Having standards for church members is not legalism. God tells us to "abstain from all appearance of evil" (I Thessalonians 5:22). How do we define all appearance of evil if we don't have any guidelines? Why would it be wrong to have standards of dress if they line up with the Bible?

In Christianity, we don't check our brains at the door and live blindly by faith. We are called to be students of the Word and can read for ourselves the biblical call to modesty. Why then are long-held standards of male and female distinction and modest dress slipping away more and more?

To make it, to really make it and thrive in our relationships with God and the people we live with in this world, we cannot simply choose to serve out of head knowledge. We can't turn off the brains God has given us and only follow our hearts. God wants us to serve Him as whole people—our minds, bodies, and spirits offered back to the Christ who continues to offer so much for us.

But what about the differences from church to church? Be at peace, my sister (Psalm 119:165) and be wise, not comparing yourself with others (II Corinthians 10:12). Remember to keep the main thing the main thing—that we cannot love the things of the world or the love of God is not in us (I John 2:15-17)—to keep *ourselves* separate from the world (II Corinthians 6:17).

If my church has fewer guidelines than the church down the street, that does not give me the right to dress immodestly. God requires all Christians to think of others before themselves. "What does the Lord require of thee? But to do justly and to love mercy and to walk humbly with thy God" (Micah 6:8).

If my church has stricter guidelines than the church down the street, I do not have the right to consider myself or my church more holy, or their church and their members less holy. The Bible says, "Who are you to judge someone else's servant? To his own master he stands or falls" (Romans 14:4, NKJV). We'll get into cultural issues in chapter 5, but for now just know it's not our call to judge our brothers and sisters or look down on them if they aren't doing things the way our pastor leads our church (Romans 14:10).

The concept of our outside lining up with our inside is a two-way street. I could be the most modest person in the church, with my clothes falling like a waterfall off my shoulders and touching nothing until they hit the ground, but if I have ugliness in my heart, it will come out and take away any positive effect my "modesty" might have had. On the outside I might look like the poster child for beauty and purity, but on the inside have a heart full of spiritual disease like pride, judging others, and backbiting.

Jesus didn't always have nice things to say about rule keepers. He spoke some hard words to the religious leaders of His day, the Pharisees. Pharisees complicated the law by adding to it, especially when it came to keeping the Sabbath. In their efforts to make sure they lived righteously, they changed God's plan of resting on the Sabbath into a chore instead of a pleasure. We can do the same thing—living joyless, rule-filled lives and losing the spiritual blessings God has provided for us. Jeremiah 31:33 tells us that God wants to put His Word in our inward parts and write them in our hearts. He wants to be our God and for us to be His people.

Jesus called the Pharisees hypocrites because they increased the burden of the law on the Israelites. They knew they couldn't keep the law themselves, yet they added even more rules to what God gave Moses. This made practicing the Jewish faith even more difficult than it already was—and it was already impossible for a mere human being.

The Old Testament Law was given to show us our need for God. No one can live up to the Law. If we could, there would have been no need for Jesus to die for our sins. God doesn't want us to pretend or be a hypocrite. His desire is to give us the real deal, a genuine holiness that comes from Him. When we seek Him with a pure heart, He will give us understanding and we will know that holiness begins in the heart.

Another thing God corrected the Pharisees about was spiritual pride (Romans 12:3). He hates spiritual pride as much as immodesty. We can fall into this way of thinking if we aren't careful. People can become proud if they think they look better than someone else. But people can also have pride in their plain appearance, considering themselves more holy than another person. In this instance, pride isn't in what is being worn on the outside, but a principle of the Bible is being violated. We are clearly instructed not to compare ourselves with others (II Corinthians 10:12).

|Now for a hard look at another question.| I've heard it asked and you probably have too. "OK. So dressing modestly pleases God, but **is it a Heaven or Hell issue?"**

First, God is the judge of every person. It would be wrong for me or anyone to assign someone to Hell. (Remember the story from chapter 3: The woman was dragged to Jesus, the only one worthy to judge her sin.) We do know that God judges people according to His Word. I am not making light of this "Heaven or Hell" question or answering it without much thought and prayer, but in my heart another question must be asked in response. What does this question say about the condition of our hearts?

If you were married and you knew something you did would disappoint your husband, would you do it on purpose anyway? Especially if you knew he would always find out about it? If you did, could you say you were acting lovingly towards your husband? Respecting him? Honoring him? Just what does a woman promise her husband on their wedding day? *Will you take this man … to love, honor, and reverence (or obey) from this time forward?*

When we become Christians, we become engaged to Jesus.

But let's take a further look at this. What married woman would ask her husband, "If I do this thing you don't like, will you divorce me?"

Do you see the similarities in this question and the original Heaven-or-Hell one? When we become Christians, we become engaged to Jesus. We are promised to Him and look forward to our marriage celebration in Heaven—Jesus and His bride—you and me. It's like a Jewish betrothal ceremony. A man and woman pledge their commitment to each other and sign their names to the agreement until the groom fulfills the terms of the agreement and returns for his wife. We entered into an agreement with God when we were born again, and now we're waiting for Him to come and fulfill the agreement. While we are waiting, will we choose to honor our commitment to our groom by living in ways that we know pleases Him?

"I work part-time as a wedding planner assistant. We do the decorating, the tuxes, and the dresses—the whole nine yards. I have never yet been to a wedding where the question was asked, 'Which one is the bride?' You simply know. Not because she is the youngest, the thinnest or even the prettiest, but because of her apparel!

"God commanded the Israelites to make fringes on their clothes and weave blue ribbons into the hems of their garments. These ribbons were visible reminders to remember God and His words, and while He gave this instruction, He told them to 'seek not after your own heart and your own eyes ... and do all my commandments' (Numbers 15:38-40). The clothes God asked the Jewish people to wear were different—they set them apart. God's people were visibly different and recognizable in whatever culture or society they lived in.

"God has always called His people to be separate from the world. We have been given a great privilege. We are His set-apart people, members of a royal priesthood, a holy nation. I hope that I am always visibly different from the world and recognizable as a follower of God. After all, I am the bride of Christ, and I want others to be able to see that without question in me."

—Amber Otwell, Odessa, Texas

The key to beauty is not what we wear on the outside, but what we carry on the inside. Everyone wants to be beautiful, but many of us are not. American icon Audrey Hepburn said, "For beautiful eyes, look for the good in others; for beautiful lips, speak only words of kindness; and for poise, walk with the knowledge that you are never alone."

"For the LORD taketh pleasure in his people: he will beautify the meek with salvation" (Psalm 149:4). The Holy Spirit inside—just being saved—will ignite a radiant glow that beautifies your life and gives glory to God.

Try This On...

Other believers may not have come to understand God's call to modesty and holiness, but that doesn't give us a pass to disobey what we know to do. Let's be examples with right spirits and walk forward, never stepping back. And remember, compromising what we know to do is not going to help us reach out to others.

Let's be examples...

Chapter Five
Does God Care about What You Wear?

|Modesty may not be your favorite topic of conversation.| You are not alone. Who wants people getting into their dresser drawers? Their closets? Even Sunday school teachers and youth leaders often avoid the subject. One reason is because talking about modesty offends some people. I don't want to offend anyone, and I'm sure you don't either, but just because something makes us squirm a bit doesn't mean we should skip over it. Modesty, although it is defined and applied differently by different people, organizations, and churches, is undoubtedly, undeniably a principle taught in the Bible—one that was followed in years past.

Jeff Pollard, Baptist pastor and author of *Christian Modesty and the Public Undressing of America,* said, **"It is not legalism to urge God's children to cover themselves, because modesty is the command of Scripture.** The desire … is to honor the Lord Jesus and to do whatever brings Him glory. … 'He that hath my commandments, and keepeth them, he it is that loveth me. … He that loveth me not keepeth not my sayings' (John 14:21, 24). The glory of God and love for Christ should be the primary motives for everything we say, do, and think, which includes what we wear."[1]

All it takes is one quick peek into history and we can see the clothing people wear today is not anywhere near the standard of decency in the not-so-distant past. In a September 12, 2003, broadcast of *20/20*, an ABC News program, a story was run on pre-teen fashion. In the teaser copy written to draw in more viewers to the program, John Stossel said, "Go to the mall these days and you'll see young girls wearing very short skirts and showing bare midriffs. Some parents call it 'hooker wear,' which is especially creepy since even eleven-year-olds wear it."

If this man recognizes that clothing styles have plunged to inappropriate and immoral standards, calling what an eleven-year-old wears "hooker wear" on national television, why are God's people so afraid to talk about it? |Well, strap on your seat belt. We are going to talk about it.|

Throughout history, immodestly exposing the body has often ended in sexual sin. The Bible makes a clear connection between nudity and sexuality.

We don't walk around nude. We should be all set then, right? That depends on who is defining the word. Let's take a look at how God defines nudity.

In addition to making garments for Adam and Eve, God gave specific dressing guidelines to His priests: "And thou shalt make them linen breeches to cover their nakedness; from the loins even unto the thighs they shall reach" (Exodus 28:42). Even though these breeches (or pants) were worn underneath their robes, this verse shows that God intended our clothing to

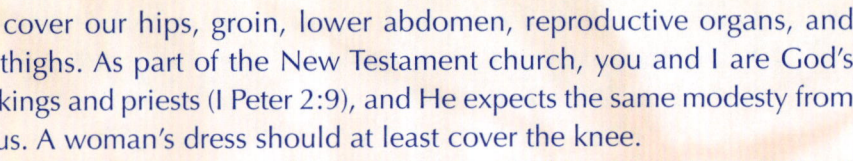

cover our hips, groin, lower abdomen, reproductive organs, and thighs. As part of the New Testament church, you and I are God's kings and priests (I Peter 2:9), and He expects the same modesty from us. A woman's dress should at least cover the knee.

Why the knee? Well, where does a thigh end? In the middle of the knee. The femur (the thigh bone) meets the tibia (the bone in the lower leg) in the middle of your kneecap, where your leg bends. To have your thigh covered, your knee should be covered beyond the halfway mark—standing or sitting.

Who's Laws? Which Laws? What Laws? Why Laws?

People say that rules without reason breed rebellion. I'm not disagreeing, but also consider that good biblical guidelines are there for good reasons—God's reasons. He created this game of life and He gets to make up the rules. We're just blessed to be on board. Still, sometimes people get confused with the different kinds of laws in the Bible—just what was done away with and what stayed the same after Jesus came. Pastor and biblical scholar David K. Bernard addressed this in his book, *Essentials of Holiness*: "The new covenant abolished (or did away with) ceremonial types, while retaining moral law and spiritual holiness."[2]

Basically, ceremonial laws of eating, drinking, and hygiene were given to the Jews and ended with Jesus. Ceremonial laws were for the Jews only, but moral laws were and are for all. Moral laws, including the Ten Commandments, are unchanging laws written by God, spoken by God, and given by

God. To break them was, and is, sin with serious consequences, even death. Ceremonial laws (you know, all those Leviticus and Deuteronomy verses) were statutes and ordinances given by Moses. Only ceremonial laws were nailed to the cross and are not necessary to follow in the New Testament relationship with God (Ephesians 2:15). **Moral laws are still in place—even strengthened by the teachings of Jesus.**

When Jesus came, He gave more than a list of rules and regulations. When He gave the Sermon on the Mount (Matthew chapters 5-7), He explained the deep spiritual concepts behind the Old Testament laws and called His followers to a higher level of obedience than rules ever could. In the Old Testament, only the physical act of adultery was wrong. In the New, Jesus said thinking lustful thoughts is equal to adultery—hatred is equal to murder. So while the ceremonial laws were done away with, all the moral laws of the Old Testament were kept and even taken up a notch.

> Now let's take a look at what the New Testament says about how Christian women should dress.
>
> "That the women adorn themselves in modest apparel, with propriety and moderation, not with braided hair or gold or pearls or costly clothing, but, which is proper for women professing godliness, with good works" (I Timothy 2:9-10, NKJV).

This book isn't a deep theological work, but we do need to look at the original meaning of the words to get the real meaning of the verse. In the original Greek, the word that is translated "dress" means a garment let down, dress, or attire, and the word for "apparel" means well-arranged, seemly, modest, of good behavior. Pick up any magazine at the grocery store and chances are you won't see any of these principles of modest dress promoted. What the world calls desirable isn't the same type of beauty God honors.

We've heard from Paul; now let's see what Peter has to say: "Your beauty should not come from outward adornment, such as braided hair and the wearing of gold jewelry and fine clothes. Instead, it should be that of your inner self, the unfading beauty of a gentle and quiet spirit, which is of great worth in God's sight" (I Peter 3:3-4, NIV).

This verse tells us we should not go to extremes in our hairdos and in the things we wear. The word *adornment* means the way we decorate ourselves, like hanging an ornament on a tree. The Bible tells us that the best things to wear do not draw attention to our outward appearance. It's not wrong to dress nice if we are moderate in our choices. **Fancying up our outer appearance is less important than beautifying (or ornamenting) our inner person.**

Fashion Rules

Lady Fashion rules so much of the world. She is a cruel dictator who demands unreasonable taxes from those who can afford to pay them and those who can't. She has the power to make us live in pain. Just think about those shoes that pinch your toes or that tummy cincher in your lingerie drawer. Fashion demands our time and attention and makes fun of those who don't follow after her. She tells us the things we wear are some of the most important things in our lives, and we can spend so much of our time and money on them that we neglect our hearts, minds, and spirits.

Even in the family of God some people try to walk as close to fashion as they can and still call themselves Christians. Some are even willing to give up their faith for no other reason than following after fashion's lusty call—like a moth to a flame, a gnat to a bug zapper, or a fish to a hook captivated by a wiggling worm.

Christians should appreciate and treasure the virtue of modesty and stand in clear contrast to those living passion-driven lives, avoiding even the appearance of impurity. "But among you there must not be even a hint of sexual immorality, or of any kind of impurity, or of greed, because these are improper for God's holy people" (Ephesians 5:3, NIV). "Not even a hint"—that's a high standard to live up to, but it's a good goal to aim for. Let's choose to stand guard for our virtue and modesty and not allow ourselves to be attracted to worldly things. Instead we should be repelled by them, like smoke from a fire keeps bugs away from our campsite.

"Turn mine eyes from beholding vanity, and quicken thou me in thy way" (Psalm 119:37). Things might have been a lot different today if Eve had turned her eyes away from things she couldn't have. Fashion magazines are tempting to look at, but it is wise to limit the time spent reading them. If you are struggling with the pull of the world, perhaps you should cut them out completely. They feed the wrong things—not your spirit, but your fleshly desires—and whatever you feed will grow. Jesus said to follow Him we must choose to give up some of the things our flesh wants—and do it every day (Luke 9:23). Yes, even on vacation. Yes, even when it's hot outside. Yes, even at a wedding or formal occasion.

More Thoughts

In Job 22:6, the Bible says, "Thou hast ... stripped the naked of their clothing." How can a naked person be stripped of their clothing? They must have had something on to be removed, but yet they were called naked. It can mean without clothes, but it also means poorly clothed or clothed in undergarments only, without an outer garment or cloak.

|What's a cloak anyway?| Science fiction books talk about cloaking devices that cause objects or people to be

partially or entirely invisible. Our outer garments, or cloaks, should make the body underneath somewhat concealed.

Revelation 3:18 tells us to buy "white raiment, that thou mayest be clothed, and that the shame of thy nakedness do not appear." In the same book, 16:15 reads, "Behold, I come as a thief. Blessed is he that watcheth, and keepeth his garments, lest he walk naked, and they see his shame." We need to pay attention to what we're wearing and doing things decently and in order.

Culture Wars and Ways

The *Zondervan Pictorial Encyclopedia of the Bible* says, "The clothing worn by the Hebrew people of biblical times was graceful, modest and exceedingly significant. ... They (the clothing) not only told who and what they were, but were intended as external symbols of the individual's innermost feelings and deepest desires and his moral urge to represent God aright."[3] Every day as they dressed, God's people were reminded that they belonged to and represented Him. As they looked at each other, their clothing reminded them to obey God's commands.

God was specific in the things He asked of the Israelites. He asked them to wear blue ribbons, symbols of His holiness, woven into their garments to remind them they were set apart to live for Him. "Speak to the children of Israel: Tell them to make tassels on the corners of their garments throughout their generations, and to put a blue thread in the tassels of the corners. And you shall have the tassel, that you may look upon it and remember all the commandments of the LORD and do them … and that you may remember and do all My commandments, and be holy for your God" (Numbers 15:38-40, NKJV).

The culture of a nation or group of people—its behaviors and beliefs, ideas and values—is seen in the lives of its people. Just like land is prepared, seeded, watered, and fertilized, the hearts of people are cultivated too. God wants us to plant His principles in our lives and develop them in ways that influence our society. We can't allow the customs of the ungodly to sweep us off our feet and allow God's culture to melt into the ways of the world.

The opposite of cultivating is ignoring or neglecting. It's easy to look at a field and know if it has been neglected or cared for. A neglected field is full of life-choking weeds instead of tended rows of nourishing fruits or vegetables. The culture of Christianity in our world will be a result of the things we, God's children, choose to cultivate in our lives.

There are many things in culture that aren't right or wrong. This book talks specifically about modesty, so let's look at an example of how culture influences dressing guidelines. In a church in North America, a woman may be asked to wear hose if she ministers on the platform. While this is an acceptable thing for a pastor to request, we have to realize that culture does play a part in issues like this. What one person might consider very important in one situation isn't always important in another. A pastor in Africa would probably not require his ladies to wear hose, and no one would think anything of it. The key is to respect the leadership in your life and follow the guidelines of your local church. Remember not to judge someone down the street or around the globe who may live with different guidelines.

Some people argue that modesty is a cultural issue—that some cultures accept nudity. But throughout the Bible, it is linked with shame. Styles of dress in American culture often draw attention to or expose body parts that were meant to remain private. As much as people don't want lines drawn for them, there are parts of our bodies that should not be put on display or emphasized by the things we wear. Instead of mirroring the look of the latest movie star, singer, or fashion designer, Christian girls can show the world a better way—one that is helpful and good, real and true, lovely and sweet.

There are real cultural wars, real battlegrounds, where we have to take a stand. The Bible gives unchanging principles that God's people must defend. The Bible tells us we should not conform to the world or love the world. It's a key theme in the Bible. "You must not do as they do in Egypt, where you used to live, and you must not do as they do in the land of Canaan, where I am bringing you. Do not follow their practices" (Leviticus 18:3, NIV). God doesn't want us to mingle with the nations and live by their customs (Psalm 106:35). **Just because a society says something is cute or OK for today, doesn't mean it is.**

Living by Principles

The Bible doesn't always give clear-cut dressing guidelines like, "three fingers below the collarbone" or "so many inches below the knee." It does give principles to follow and truths to obey. Although it doesn't always spell everything out, the Bible always gives dependable principles to live by. You won't read, "Thou shalt not watch MTV" but you can read, "I will set no wicked thing before mine eyes" (Psalm 101:3).

Scripture doesn't say, "Women shalt not wear pants." There were no women's pants in those days for prophets or disciples to write about, although men wore linen breeches under their robes. But can we take an honest look at the concept of modesty? Can we look at what the Bible calls naked and clothed in comparison to what modern society says is acceptable? If we are honest enough to take a look, and our hearts are open enough to receive the concepts, will we be willing to obey—even if it is against our culture? When we belong to Jesus, we live in God's culture!

Cupping Concept

A lot of prayer has been lifted for this book project. The team working on it really sought the Lord for the right words to transmit biblical concepts in ways any woman or girl could apply when she goes to her closet or the department store dressing room. In prayer, a Scripture verse came to mind and with it an idea called the "cupping concept."

"Therefore, I urge you, brothers, in view of God's mercy, to offer your bodies as living sacrifices, holy and pleasing to God—this is your spiritual act of worship. Do not conform any longer to the pattern of this world, but be transformed by the renewing of your mind. Then you will be able to test and approve what God's will is—His good, pleasing and perfect will" (Romans 12:1-2, NIV).

As I read that verse, the word *conform* popped off the page. We are not to conform to the pattern of the world. Funny how it all ties together. Patterns are used to make clothes, right? God's Word says, "do not conform." It may seem just a play on words, but let's look at this. According to *Merriam-Webster's Online Dictionary* conform means:

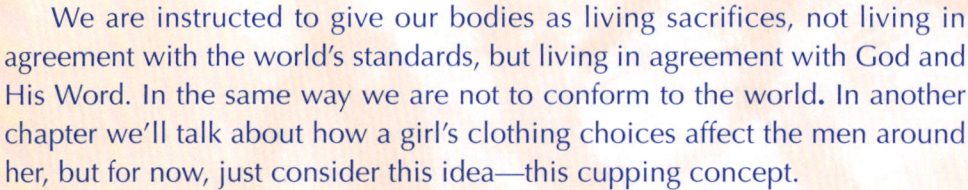

- to give the same shape, outline, or contour to
- to be similar or identical
- to be obedient or compliant
- to act in accordance with prevailing standards or customs[4]

We are instructed to give our bodies as living sacrifices, not living in agreement with the world's standards, but living in agreement with God and His Word. In the same way we are not to conform to the world. In another chapter we'll talk about how a girl's clothing choices affect the men around her, but for now, just consider this idea—this cupping concept.

Adam and Eve's clothes probably didn't have darts and tucks that molded them to their bodies, and for sure they weren't lycra stretch-o-matics. The clothes we wear should clearly indicate we are women without revealing all the details of our private feminine parts. In I Corinthians 12:23, Paul says the indecent parts of the body actually receive more honor and attention to modesty. There is an inborn sense of shame that leads us to cover our private places, but that shame is not a bad thing. That sense of shame shows respect for parts of the body meant to be kept concealed. The negative shame comes when we show private things in public, and we can show their shape very plainly at the same time they are completely covered with fabric. I call it that "vacuum sealed" look.

> "She looked as if she had been poured into her clothes and had forgotten to say when."
> – P. G. Wodehouse, English writer

We can have all the body parts covered, but not appropriately concealed, like that hidden treasure we talked about in chapter 2. The same Hebrew word translated "concealment" also means "virgin or unmarried."

If a pirate "buried" a three-foot-tall treasure chest in a one-foot-deep hole and covered the part sticking out of the shallow hole with a layer of dirt, that treasure chest would not be hidden, just covered. Everyone would know exactly where it was. In the same way, tight clothes that cup body parts are not modest, regardless of how much flesh they cover. If people can see your rib cage rise and fall with every breath and your veins and other various bodily lumps and bumps through your clothes, it's time to change.

Women look at women differently than men look at women. When women wear clothing that outlines their shape, like tight or low-cut shirts, clingy dresses or pants, **their female anatomy is revealed, even though it is covered.** Even a sweet-looking skirt hemmed well below the knee can be very immodest if it swells around the buttocks or follows the curve of the hips and thighs like so many of today's mermaid-style skirts. Personally, I'm glad we don't live in the era of hoopskirts or petticoats and all the layers women used to wear, but we still need to be aware of the way fabric falls from the hips down.

Gender Distinction – Telling the Boys from the Girls

Although there has been the occasional rebel throughout history, every culture has maintained dressing distinctions between guys and girls. Missionary Linda Y. Reed wrote in *Subconscious Sexual Signals* that "only in Communist cultures was this distinction abolished." Even in societies where women wore pant-like clothes, they still covered their thighs with flowing tunics or long skirts worn over them.

Deuteronomy 22:5 is an important Scripture verse on dressing for gender distinction: "The woman shall not wear that which pertaineth unto a man, neither shall a man put on a woman's garment: for all that do so are abomination unto the LORD thy God."

There are just some things God does not change His mind about. "For I am the LORD, I change not" (Malachi 3:6).

|Why is gender distinction so important?| God made men and women different by His design, and He doesn't want the clothing we put on our bodies to cause gender confusion. God's strong reaction to cross-dressing

tells us that what a woman wears should be obviously different, from the very first look. In the Bible, robes were worn by men and women, but the way they were made left no doubt as to their sex. In our Western society and culture, women are identified by a skirt or dress. If you don't believe me, just look on any public restroom door. When it comes right down to it, it's nice to be a girl, don't you think? Comedian Gilda Radner said, "I'd much rather be a woman than a man. Women can cry, they can wear cute clothes, and they're the first to be rescued off sinking ships." Sometimes it just pays to be a girl.

Pants

The Bible calls pants "breeches," and these were worn only by men for close to six thousand years of human existence. In Bible days men and women wore long robes and men sometimes wore shorter ones over breeches that went down to the knees. Whenever a man's robe got in the way of his work, he pulled up the edge and tucked it into his breeches. This is what the Bible calls "girding up your loins" and it is something only men did. "Gird up now thy loins like a man; for I will demand of thee, and answer thou me" (Job 38:3).

Scripture, along with our cultural history, backs up the basis for the old question, "Who wears the pants in the family?" The answer is supposed to be the man. Why does wearing the pants mean acting like a man? Women in our society did not commonly wear pants until the mid-1900s. That's not that long ago girls, compared to the history of the world. Let's look at how the change came about.

In 1850 feminist Amelia Bloomer introduced short dresses (still below the knee) worn over full pants often gathered at the ankle. The public responded with outrage and people dressed pretty much the same until the rebellious Roaring Twenties. During World War I skirt hems rose, and women forced to

work in factories began wearing more masculine apparel on their jobs. Everywhere else they wore dresses and skirts. After the war, women began wearing pants in public and just a few short decades later, in the 1960s, miniskirts, bra burning, and free love were a way of life. That's an amazingly quick breakdown of morality, and the decline began when women started wearing pants. Of course there are many factors involved in this decline, but the base of the downward spiral was women taking on men's roles which resulted in a change in their clothing. This eventually changed our society, and not all for the better.

Have you ever noticed how girls in pants sit and act in more masculine ways than girls in skirts and dresses? It's undeniable. When we wear a skirt or dress, we almost always act more feminine. Italian designer Donatella Versace disapproved of presidential candidate Hillary Clinton's choice of clothing. "I can understand (trousers) are comfortable but she's a woman and she … should treat femininity as an opportunity and not try to emulate masculinity," Versace said.

In today's society, so many people have grown up wearing pants that they don't understand the association with men's apparel. If our society now says pants are OK to wear, and even makes special women's pants, why bother living according to customs of the past? In the church we hear a lot of talk about keeping to the old paths, but to a young person, that might not sound so appealing. We want to be here and now, not back in the "old days."

"I am a registered nurse. Most nurses wear scrubs. When I started nursing school there were two choices in scrubs: a purple top and pants or a purple top with a white skirt. I never doubted what I would do and faithfully wore my purple top and white skirt. Since I attended a Christian university, not many people doubted my choice or reasons for doing so. My peers and instructors knew me and my beliefs.

"When I first joined the workforce I worked at a large Catholic-based hospital and made sure my uniform of a scrub skirt and top would be acceptable. At every place I have worked, no employer has said otherwise. When I first became a real nurse I did have questions. I wondered if I would be immodest at times wearing a skirt—if I would be in situations where my skirt might be revealing. I also wondered if God would approve of me wearing a scrub top and pants just for work-related purposes. The conviction I came to was that I could not wear the pants because doing so would take away from my witness. If I could not be myself, living out the full testimony of God's grace in my life, I would feel like a hypocrite.

"My self-esteem is higher, knowing I have followed through on my convictions, and I have had patients and fellow nurses tell me I look like a real nurse. I am careful not to place myself in positions that could be immodest. I wear support hose and my skirts are all below the knee while allowing enough movement for me to fully perform my duties modestly and respectfully while keeping my convictions intact."

– Elda M. Luera, R.N., B.S.N., Port Lavaca, Texas

The old paths aren't good because they are old; they are good because they are tried and proven. If something in you rebels against the "old paths," think of them as the tried and true paths. God in His wisdom has set guardrails along the way. **These guardrails, or guidelines, aren't the road or the bridge we walk on, but they keep us safe** as we walk on the path of life to our ultimate destination—Heaven with Jesus.

Some people argue that pants are more comfortable than skirts. Our comfort should never be more important than pleasing God and obeying His Word. Jesus probably wasn't very comfortable on the cross. As far as comfort goes, slip on some boots and some cozy tights under your skirt in the winter, and you'll be warm. And in the summer, what could be cooler than a lightweight skirt and sandals? A dress really isn't an uncomfortable garment.

Beyond biblical definitions, history, and customs, the fact remains that pants are just not modest. The lower anatomy may be covered with fabric, but pants accentuate body parts and reveal far more detail of a woman's body than a skirt. Pants draw attention to a woman's figure. Even loose fitting pants outline a woman's feminine shape. It's just the make-up of pants in general, if not while standing, definitely when sitting or bending. And I have yet to see a "modest" pair of jeans.

Pants cup the buttocks—there's that cupping concept again. And when women wear clothes that cup their private body parts, men's eyes are drawn to things they shouldn't be: the shape of thighs, hips, and crotch that tempt them to impure thoughts. It's been confirmed by psychologists and it's just common sense. (See Linda Reed's *Subconscious Sexual Signals*.[5])

A little common sense and a lot of loving God and others can go a long way in helping us understand the difference between right and wrong. It also helps us remember the effect our choices have on those around us. A not-too-tight skirt or dress that covers the knee is the best choice to properly cover the shape of your lower body.

My Choice, My Rights

Of course it is an adult's choice to dress how they choose to dress and a young person's too—within their parent's guidelines. God has given each of us free choice, but with the choices come consequences. The truth is, **although we do have choice, we don't really have the right to dress as we please** in ways that feed our pride and stimulate sensuality in ourselves and others.

Whether dressing carefully, carelessly, or blatantly rebellious, the clothes we wear affect the way we feel about ourselves and the people around us. We have the power to tear down or build up. As God's girls, we are called to consider others, live moderate lives, and glorify Him in our bodies. If our bodies belong to God, we are responsible to clothe them in ways that please Him.

We can learn a Bible lesson from algebra, a type of equation. If $a=b$ then $c(a)=c(b)$. If covering = godly, then uncovering = ungodly. Think about the demon-possessed man in Luke, chapter 8. Demons made this poor guy tear his clothes off and run around naked; but when Jesus brought deliverance, people were amazed to find him clothed and in his right mind. One demon-possessed man tore the clothes off seven men (Acts 19:16). It looks like the devil has a thing against clothes!

Remember, covering is more than just physical clothing on our bodies. There is a spiritual dimension involved. If we love God, we obey His Word. When we submit to the Word of God, we will practice modesty. When we practice modesty, we are physically covered, and that is an outward sign of our spiritual covering and protection. If you're in the process of developing a modest heart, why don't you ask for some input from someone older and wiser who can help? An older woman can give good counsel since they've seen seasons of fashion come and go.

What Not to Wear

We've talked about a lot of this already, but here are some extra thoughts on the subject of what not to wear. Like it or not, the Bible says that certain clothing identifies a prostitute. "Then out came a woman to meet him, dressed like a prostitute" (Proverbs 7:10, NIV).

Not one person reading this book would appreciate her wardrobe being labeled "hooker wear." Neither would she sign up for the leading role in a porn movie or center spread in a girly magazine. But if we wear seductive clothes, the end result is similar. We stimulate lust in the men around us, and we bear the blame for our actions. We are not innocent, even if we are virgins.

Lust for money and clothing has caused a lot of trouble through the years. Achan's entire family and his cattle lost their lives (Joshua 7). Gehazi was struck with leprosy (II Kings 5). Our own lusts can draw us away from God (James 1:13-15). **If we allow the Bible to set our boundaries it will show us the way.** God's Word will give us the motivation and power to cleanse our flesh and our spirits (II Corinthians 7:1).

> "Many come to bring their clothes to church rather than themselves."
> – Thomas Fuller, 17th Century English Clergyman

According to the writings of Paul and Peter, clothing should not be overly expensive. Beyond feeding our pride, it's not good stewardship. The foreign missions division reports that for every penny invested, a gospel tract can be printed. How many lost people could we reach with money we have spent on extravagant clothes, shoes, purses, and hair accessories? How many starving children could be fed? Colossians 3:1-5 tells us to set our hearts on things above—not to be absorbed in ourselves. Jesus said to deny ourselves and follow Him. If we really seek to live for God, we will be willing to listen when He points out areas in our lives that need a little polishing.

Try This On...

The ultimate clothing choice is to put on Christ (Galatians 3:27). When we do that, we should put on the mind of Christ, which is to do the will of the Father. Jesus had a modest spirit, and a modest spirit will result in modest dress, appropriate and sensible.

> "I was actually in the first grade when God told me not to wear pants or shorts anymore. I didn't understand all that meant, but I went to my mom crying because I felt the presence of God. I told her what I felt and heard, and I never wore pants or shorts again. Shortly after that we began attending a church that taught modesty. God had already prepared me for this change, and I thank Him for that."
>
> —Becky Verdula, Wheeling, West Virginia

Chapter Six
Fashion Statements

|This is the life-gets-real chapter| written to help you make good choices when it comes time to reach inside your closet or dresser drawers. Before we get into the helpful hints, remember that men are visually sensitive. When a girl dresses immodestly, she tempts the men around her to sin; but when she dresses modestly, men are free to enjoy her feminine beauty without added sexual temptation. You, daughter of the King, are free to be lovely, but not to stir up lustful thoughts in yourself or others—pretty, but not provocative.

Have you ever fasted? Imagine you haven't eaten all day. You walk in the door of your home and discover someone has just baked chocolate chip cookies. Your nostrils flare at the smell and your mouth immediately starts moistening. You shake your head to dispel the sweet aroma teasing and taunting your senses. "I've got to get out of here," you mumble under your breath before you dash through the kitchen. Once in your room, the smell is still heavy in the air. You find a plate of warm cookies on your nightstand next to a steaming cup of Starbucks just the way you like it. "Oh, God, help me!" You run to the bathroom and slam the door. "How am I supposed to do without cookies when I see them everywhere I turn?" Well, girls, you are the cookies, and the guys are the fasters, and we need to help them out. OK? OK! Let's dress lovely and lovingly and help our brothers in the Lord keep their thoughts pure.

Our clothes should be appropriate for the occasion, attractive, clean, and neat. Loretta Young, an actress famous for her beauty, fashion, and grace said, "Wearing the correct dress for any occasion is a matter of good manners." Time for another equation: **Homeliness does not equal holiness.** Just look around at the world God made and you will see He must love beautiful things. Being modest doesn't mean being frumpy or purposely trying to look unattractive. We don't dress drab for Jesus! He likes color and flowers and textures. The trick is to keep a good balance between dreary starkness and drippy showiness. Speaking of color, Greek philosopher Diogenes of Sinope said, "Modesty is the color of virtue." A pretty thought, isn't it?

You are free to be yourself in your choice of color and style. There is nothing wrong with wearing pretty clothes. God made women attractive on purpose, and His Word does not teach us to wear dull colors or sloppy styles. And while we're getting ready to make our appearance in the world, we should certainly pay attention to our hygiene and grooming as well as what we are wearing.

"I was recently in a department store and I noticed a lady watching me. As I started toward the checkout counter, she stepped over in front of me, smiled, and said, 'I just have to tell you that you look absolutely radiant and confident. And I love the way you are dressed.' People do notice.

"Three of us from the office went out for lunch one day. An elderly gentleman opened the door for us as we left and asked, 'Do you ladies dress this way all the time?' A little surprised, we answered, 'Yes.' He said, 'It has been a long time since I have seen women in general dress this way—as a matter of fact, since just after World War II. You rarely see it anymore.' If you study history, that's the time women began to openly wear pants and that changed the mode of dress completely in just a few short years. The Bible tells us to seek and ask for the old paths. Purity is a path worth taking. Let's take it!"

—Gwyn Oakes,
Bald Knob, Arkansas

You can have your own personal style and still be a saint of the Most High God on your way to glory, glory, hallelujah. It's OK to be fashionable as long as you aren't a slave to fashion. Your style is an expression of yourself, your own dressing language—one way of communicating with the world a bit about yourself without saying a word. Have you considered what your dressing language says about you? Marlene Dietrich, the actress credited with first wearing pants in a movie, said she did not dress for herself, the public, or for men. She said, "I dress for the image." We all convey an image, and what we wear should identify us with godly people, not the ungodly.

He Says, She Says . . .

So you're out shopping with your bff (that means best friend forever for you moms out there). You're in the dressing room with some cute stuff to try on. Here are some questions to ask yourself before you buy:

1. Do I love it—on and off the hanger?
2. Does it follow biblical standards of modesty and femininity?
3. Is there anything questionable about it?
4. Could it be a stumbling block or cause impure thoughts in the guys around me?
5. Can I afford it?
6. Is this the image I want to project?
7. Does it complement who I am as a person or does it take away from it?
8. Does it bring honor and glory to God?

Before you take your bff's advice and buy that new outfit, make sure you are both on the same page with dressing guidelines. American fashion designer

Geoffrey Beene said, "A woman should be less concerned about Paris and more concerned about whether the dress she's about to buy relates to the way she lives." Ultimately, the decision is yours to buy clothes that line up with your principles. Before you do the undoable and take the tag off, you might want to run your new purchase by your dad. He'll let you know if something his little pumpkin is wearing is not up to par.

Shopping for modest clothes can get frustrating, especially in the juniors' section, but don't give up. Keep on looking until you find something you like that reflects your love for God, others, and yourself.

Praise the Lord!

The PTL Test

To take the Praise the Lord test, raise your hands to the ceiling like you're giving God some praise. Check your reflection in the mirror. Is your midriff or back exposed? Did your hemline rise above your knee? Next, touch your toes like you're bowing in worship. Check the mirror again from all angles. Anything showing from the top, waist, or bottom, front or back that shouldn't be? If not, you've passed the PTL test. Hallelujah!

The Silhouette Test

Standing sideways in front of a full-length mirror, check to see if your feminine shape is revealed by clothes that are too tight. When people look at you, they should see your clothing, not every curve of your body on display. We can provocatively expose our shapes even when we're completely covered—that's why tight clothes are called "revealing." Remember that cupping concept, front and back. Clothing, especially in church, should be Rated G, and you and the guys around you should both be able to breathe when you're wearing them.

Top Talk

- We've already discussed that our shirts shouldn't be too tight. Also be careful with loose-fitting tops or shirts with scoop necks. Layering a tighter garment underneath is a good way to make sure you don't expose yourself when you're on the move.

- Check for gaps between buttonholes. To fix gaps, sew snaps between the buttons, pin them closed, or wear the top open with a layer underneath.

- In order to properly cover the trunk of the body as we discussed in chapter 2, all shirts need to have sleeves. Remember, you're going to be moving around and people will see you from all angles. Shirts without adequate sleeves can be a peep show waiting to happen. Be careful with loose or bell sleeves for the same reason. You may want to wear a shirt of a matching fabric to line the arm under these types of sleeves.

- When wearing knits (t-shirts and sweaters), show some extra care with clingy material. Knits made "sweater girls" famous in Hollywood in the 1940s when actresses wore tight sweaters to emphasize their bustlines and advertise the latest in brassiere development.

- Don't compromise modesty for a proper fit in the shoulders. Keep looking until you find what works for you. Busty gals may want to go with a layer over knits so they can get a smaller size button-down shirt or jacket that fits properly at the shoulders.

- Be careful with empire waistlines that gather near or just under the bust and halter styles that cup the breasts individually. These styles unavoidably draw attention to the bustline.

- Tube tops, not usually topping the list of modest apparel, can add some variety to the clothes you are able to wear and still be modest. Pull one on and wear it high under a shirt with a low neckline, or slip one around your waist under a short top. The extra fabric will cover what the designer neglected to.

- When you buy a shirt that doesn't have a button high enough to cover all it should, take one of the extra ones provided by the manufacturer or take one off the bottom. Either make a buttonhole and sew on the button, or for those who don't do buttonholes, sew the button on the same side as the buttonholes (not the buttons) then safety-pin the top behind the button after you put it on.

Skirting the Issue

We've covered this pretty thoroughly, but how about some helpful hints?

- Skirt hems should be below the knee when sitting, standing, bending, or raising hands. For your comfort, choose skirts that aren't daringly short so you won't have to fuss with them when you sit down or stand up.

- Remember, no cupping hips, thighs, or buttocks. The seams and design of the skirt should at the very least have the fabric fall straight from the hips or fuller, not tapering in.

- When buying a skirt, sit down facing the front of the mirror and see how it looks. Give some honest consideration to how comfortable you are going to be while you are sitting in it. Remember, you're going to have to move around too. Beyond sitting and standing, you will likely be getting in and out of your car and walking up steps. Make sure your legs are covered from every angle, and be careful about how you bend,

because a skirt that is completely modest when standing can rise way up in the back if you lean over. It's best to bend at the knees.

- If you wear skirts with slits, you have to check two hemlines: the bottom of the skirt and the top of the slit. A good way to tell if your slit is too high is to answer this question. Pin your skirt up all around where the slit begins and check the mirror. Does your length still cover your knees (front and back)? Many slits can be slip-stitched without too much work, and a seamstress can do a great job taking the side seams out and bringing the slit to a decent length or getting rid of the slit altogether. Some slits can be filled with fabric or even bonded closed with an iron-on adhesive.

- If you know you'll be active, make sure you're not wearing a straight skirt with no give. You won't be able to move or sit properly. Remember to keep your knees together when you're sitting and conduct yourself with dignity and femininity regardless of what you are wearing.

- If you love a skirt but it's just too short, you can add a band of complementary or contrasting fabric or wide ribbon or lace to the hem. This can be very tailored, chic, or feminine-looking according to your tastes. You can also cut a strip of fabric from the hem, add a band of contrasting fabric and sew the bottom piece back on for a color-block affect.

If you have a skirt that is part of a suit or one you will be wearing under a long top, fabric can be added at the waist. This might be a bit challenging for some, or even require hiring a seamstress to help, but if you need professional clothing or an outfit for a special occasion, it's a great idea.

 If you don't have a personal conviction or pastoral direction about wearing culottes, these can be worn for active wear as long as they are loose fitting, skirt-like, and modest—not just baggy basketball shorts from the men's department. We know what modest is by now, right? No cupping cheeky body parts or outlining thighs, hips, or

> "In the church I grew up in, girls would tug at their dresses because they were so short and when they sat, they would put a small towel over their knees. I personally want to be comfortable and stay modest at the same time. If I am constantly having to tug at my clothing because I know it is too short or too revealing, I don't think I should be wearing it."
>
> –Dawn Weber, Plainfield, Indiana

crotch. The hem should be the same as what is acceptable for your skirts. Keep in mind your activity may cause some fabric swinging, and you should be covered in whatever position you may end up in.

 If you're really passionate about a sport like skiing, there are patterns and people available to make ski skirts and other active wear. Check the Internet for more information.

A Tip from The Top

"When I find a skirt I like and it has a slit, I take it to the fabric shop and match it as closely as possible. I then add a kick pleat in the slit area.

"Once I found a gorgeous skirt with a slit up the front that went halfway up my thighs. It was gray and had a one-inch strip of black leather on either side that continued to where the strips joined at the waist. I found a piece of material the same shade as the leather and added a five-fold pleat in the slit. Now absolutely no one has a skirt like it! This is very easy to do if you sew, and if you don't, a seamstress can do it for you."

—Gwyn Oakes, Ladies Ministries president

Keep in mind, most of us do have our dressing challenges. For the busty, for the not-so busty, the petite, the tall, the apple-shaped, the pear-shaped—we all have to pay attention and take the time to make the right decisions based on our bodies, not what someone else can wear on theirs, and still be modest.

> **Jesus is the Good Shepherd and we are His sheep. Sheep should look like sheep and not a sheep in wolf's clothing—or a wolf in sheep's clothing.**

Undercover Agents

We've already discussed how what we wear on the outside is a reflection of who we are on the inside, but what about that middle ground? What about those very private garments—the ones we find in the intimates department?

Intimate apparel. Hmmm. Just the name bears some consideration. What makes underclothing *intimate*? Perhaps because these items cover our most private parts.

> **Did you ever wonder what guys are really thinking? A recent survey taken anonymously by 1,600 young men of differing Christian denominations revealed some startling statistics. Young women wrote the questions, and the complete survey is available at *http://www.therebelution.com/modestysurvey*.[1]**

Seeing "London and France" would make a lovely European holiday; however, it's an embarrassing scenario that takes place all too often on the streets of America.

|Revelation 16:15| tells believers to watch and keep their garments. In addition to our outer clothing, every woman, young and old, should carefully consider her selection of foundation garments. God doesn't want us to be care*less* dressers, but care*ful*. **Under garments should never become outer garments.**

Are bra straps (or more) peeking out of your top? One sixteen-year-old surveyed said that seeing bra straps, even when unintentional on the part of a girl, "invites the mind to wander below the shirt and wonder what the rest looks like." Of those taking the modesty survey, 69 percent reported that seeing a girl reach inside her shirt to adjust a bra strap is a stumbling block.

Remember: Safety pins are your friends!

If a top opening gapes, layer a tank or simple knit shirt underneath. For renegade straps that just won't stay in place, pin those straps to the tank and forget having to tuck them in for the rest of the day. Fumbling with straps is distracting for everybody.

How about those bottoms? If you like low-rise waistbands, make sure you're covered. When you tuck in a tank or simple knit top, you can wear the style waistband you like without exposing your panties or abdomen when you move. |You can have your style and keep your virtue.|

Is sheer clothing revealing bras and panties underneath? First, if it's very sheer, it's just got to go—but some fabrics are suitable given a little attention to detail.

As cute as today's variety of colored and patterned undergarments are, not every item is suitable for every outfit. Keep some flesh-colored bras and panties on hand (white shows through), especially in the summer when wearing light fabrics. |And don't slip up and forget to wear a slip.| For some outfits they are a must!

Is your clothing so form-fitting that people see outlines of bras and panties when you're standing or moving? Of the young men surveyed, 75 percent said lines of undergarments visible under clothing caused them to stumble.

More than articles of clothing are in question if this is happening. Modesty goes beyond simply concealing underwear, skin, and body parts. It's about keeping the mystery of your feminine shape for that one special man who will delight in the fact that you did.

Remember the cupping concept and be not conformed. Embrace the mystery of modesty. Respect your femininity and the way it affects others by choosing *not* to wear outfits that reveal everything but your mother's maiden name.

Modesty goes beyond what you wear on the outside. It is an internal, foundational issue of attitude and heart. If our thoughts are modest (not attention-grabbing *look-at-me* or *I-have-sexual-power* attitudes), we will not desire to wear articles of clothing that promote sensuality.

Dressing provocatively, even if it's just our private undergarments, takes a step away from purity. Although intimate apparel is not worn on the outside, what we wear beneath the surface layer definitely has the power to promote feelings of sensuality. Our undergarments affect the way we feel about ourselves, and this transmits to those around us.

Scripture reveals in |Jeremiah 6:15 and 8:12| that God's people can become desensitized to the point we lose our ability to blush or feel proper remorse when we should be ashamed. We should be concerned when Christian young ladies are unashamed or unembarrassed when boundaries of modest dress are crossed.

A Few Finer Points

Are you cold? Or are your body parts indicating you are?

Prepare for potentially embarrassing situations by wearing a bra with a proper lining, especially if your shirt is on the thinner side. Layering may help, but if this is a recurring problem, you might consider padded inserts.

Are you active? Proper undergarments for physical activities is important. Of the young men surveyed, 77 percent reported seeing a girl's chest bounce when she walks or runs is a stumbling block.

Consider doubling up when you're exercising. Some girls wear sports bras layered with a second supportive bra to help keep things in check. And by all means, forgo clingy t-shirts that accentuate every jiggle. If you are extremely active, you might consider wearing tight-fitting lining garments that hide thighs and abdomens that may inadvertently be uncovered when you dive for a volleyball or hang from the monkey bars.

Are you a full-figured girl? It's challenging enough to find modest clothing in the stores, but for the full-figured girl, the task is even more difficult.

You may just have to bite the bullet and go for a minimizer. Sure, they aren't as cutesy as some of the slingshot varieties, but they will free a fuller-breasted girl to wear a greater variety of clothing on the outside—clothes that lie nicely, don't gape, or draw undue attention to anything other than her lovely face.

Are you a girly girl? Of the young men participating in the modesty survey, 66 percent said the lacy lingerie look of some tops is a stumbling block and 51 percent said lace edges sticking out of the tops of shirts look too much like underwear.

Does this mean Christian women should not wear lace-edged tops? Lace is fine, as long as it doesn't make your top look like lingerie. Consider lining behind the lace so your top doesn't look like a nighty. Applying a strip of fabric or ribbon with iron-on tape can make this a quick and painless venture.

Try This On...

Catch this: In the core of every heart is a desire to be treated with **dignity** and **respect.** The way we choose to dress, speak, and conduct ourselves causes others to respond in ways that affirm our dignity and worth as godly Christian women.

dignity and respect

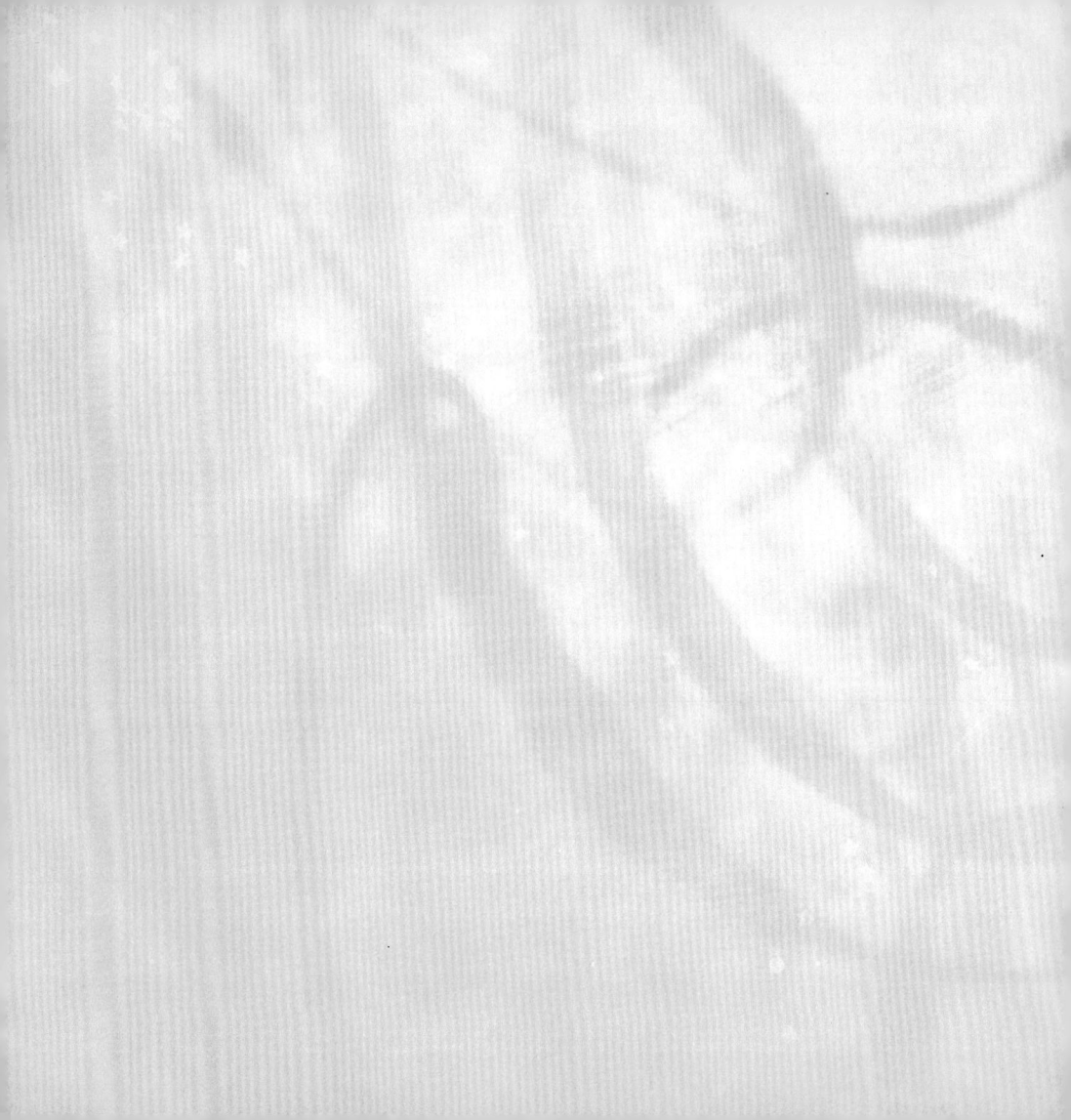

Chapter Seven
The Mystery of Modesty and the Protective Power of Purity

"Modesty wasn't popular in the school I attended. There were no uniforms, and, although there was some kind of a dress code, it was never strictly followed. I saw tight jeans, mini-skirts, and tiny tops. I could see flesh, flesh, flesh. These were the girls who were the most popular and got lots of attention. What was the lesson I learned? Well, isn't it obvious? A girl has to show all she has in order to become popular and get attention. At that moment, I didn't think much of the true nature of the attention girls like these receive, and it didn't occur to me that by putting emphasis on their bodies, they actually said, 'There is nothing more in me than this. I am my body.'

"It wasn't all about clothes, either; it was about conduct. Speaking loudly, flirting, cursing, walking provocatively—it was all very common. I did the same. I wore tight clothes, showed off my legs, shoulders, and midriff. I flirted, I was provocative—and I received attention and looks as I walked down the streets. Needless to say, I owned very few skirts in those days, and those I had were far above my knees.

"The way you dress reflects the way you think. Dressing in a certain manner will almost undoubtedly have an impact on your life. It breaks my heart to say this, but when I was still very young, I got involved in a meaningless, promiscuous relationship that was based solely on physical attraction and lust. No surprises here—if a young girl doesn't bring out her mind and soul, but shows off her flesh, she will only get the men who want her body. They will swarm around her, like flies around a jar of honey, and none of them will be interested in what she thinks or has to say.

"I am not going to elaborate right now about the promiscuity I was involved in. Unsurprisingly, it ended in heartbreak. So, what happened next?

"Suddenly, almost instinctively, I wrapped myself in long, loose, and dark clothes—

shabby, shapeless skirts and jumpers. They were mostly old and ill-fitting, but I didn't want to wear anything else. It was like trying to protect myself from anything that might hurt me again by covering every inch of my body. No one looked at me on the street anymore. My heart was bruised and bleeding for many months.

"It was a time of intense, painful personal growth and change. And among many other things, I realized something very important: The feeling of protection I experienced upon covering everything that used to be revealed wasn't an illusion. Covering my body protected me from those who wanted only my body. I sent a different message to the world now.

"Of course, at that point I was dressed modestly, but very unattractively. The next step, after initial healing and understanding what had happened to me, was acquiring a flattering, cheerful, feminine, and modest wardrobe. From that moment on, I intended to dress in a way that was attractive, not *attracting*. I wanted to dress in a manner that would say, 'I respect my body and my physical attractiveness, but the most important thing about me is my soul, and it's not something I am going to reveal to just anyone.'

"Today, I experience a wonderful sense of being on the right track. I received an outstanding blessing, a feeling of someone taking me by the hand and leading me from darkness to light. Modesty in both conduct and manner of dressing, as I found out, sends a message of respect to everyone around me—and as a logical outcome, I get respect in return.

"If there is one thing I would like to say to other young ladies, it is this: You are lovely young women. You are more, much more, than your bodies. Respect yourself and others. Showing off your bodies will only get you the wrong type of attention from the wrong men. A lovely, long, flowing skirt and a pretty, modest shirt will not only bring out your beauty; they will protect you from being used and abused."

–Anna S.

|There is a mystery to feminine charm|—something that connects the visible and the invisible. Women have a source of power in their sexuality, and that power is not a toy to be played with. It is a gift from God. We can corrupt this gift and use it to manipulate and control others for our pleasure and benefit, or we can choose to honor God and His Word. **When we make godly choices, we have real power:** power to keep ourselves and others from falling into sin; power to live holy and pure for the God who loves us and gave Himself for us.

Akhenaton, a pharaoh who lived in fourteenth century BC said, "When virtue and modesty enlighten her charms, the luster of a beautiful woman is brighter than the stars of Heaven, and the influence of her power it is in vain to resist." That's pretty powerful, don't you think? Even an Egyptian king can't resist the influence of a virtuous and modest woman.

Christian author C. S. Lewis said, "How little people know who think that holiness is dull. When one meets the real thing … it is irresistible." In some ways, women lead men, and we need to be responsible leaders. What women have allowed and refused to allow have had major influence on society.

A balanced walk between extreme nitpicky legalism and excessive sinful indulgence is the only path of true freedom. Legalism and indulgence are both forms of bondage, but God wants us to walk in liberty. The truly liberated Christian woman has a quality that others see and it draws them to her. She is free from society's revolving, evolving, flip-flopping fashions and standards—free to live safe inside the protection and blessings of modesty and purity.

Modesty encourages men to act with honor, to be gentlemen. Modesty protects a woman's vulnerability, and we are weaker than men. I like it when my door is opened or my package carried. This courteous behavior happens more often when women are dressed like women, clothed with dignity.

Modesty is a stop sign, a defensive line that guards purity and puts out potential fires sparked by provocative clothing. Dressing with discretion, using wisdom and good judgment, is your choice. You have the power to choose, and that power affects the way others think about you and behave around you.

Today women wear in public what would have been called "underwear" not so long ago. They are then surprised that the rate of sexual assaults and date rapes has risen to astronomical proportions. It is always wrong for a girl to be violated in any way, verbally or physically, but when women dress in ways that keep men constantly stimulated, those boiling pots may bubble over. Perhaps our self-indulgent, sensual society is not entirely blameless.

"I feel protected by modesty. It's an outward sign, not only to the world but the enemy (and also to myself), that I live this faith and I live this relationship with God on a daily basis. It stops me from reacting sometimes in ways that aren't the best witness because it reminds me that I am different.

"Modesty is also like a boundary that keeps back rebellion. If I were to let down my guard on my modesty, what would be the next guard I would let down? I don't even want to know.

"Modesty also protects us from vanity. It keeps us humble and at the same times boosts our confidence. Our bodies are something that God has given us that we have control over. We decide who passes our boundaries and how far they're allowed to go.

"Wearing modest clothing, I am free! I am free from the fads and trends of this world. I am free to dress comfortably and femininely and to dress to please the love of my life, my Lord and Savior."
—Amanda Reed, Williamsburg, Michigan

Think about it like this. If you're in high school, you put a lock on your locker. If you have a car, you lock it when you get out (at least city girls do). When you leave your house, you lock the front door and at bedtime you deadbolt it. Why? To protect the things inside. If you left your car unlocked and something was stolen or damaged, it would be wrong, it would be a disappointment, but should it be a surprise? Our bodies are much more precious than our book bags, stereos, and personal belongings and we protect them when we keep our entrances sealed.

Have you ever passed a house at night with the curtains wide open and the lights on? It's like looking in a fish bowl. There is something mesmerizing about it and you just can't help looking inside. The same thing happens when we dress in ways we shouldn't. We all know it's not polite to look, but there's something in us that just gapes, even if we're women, even if we do it discreetly.

A modestly dressed woman helps the men around her live pure lives, but it also protects her. She shuts the door to lustful spirits that dressing sensually invites into the lives of women who dress in slinky, sexy clothes—lustful spirits and their own carnal desires that stir up sensual feelings and make them more vulnerable to falling into sin.

Modesty protects sexual purity for both girls and guys. As we discussed in chapter 2, God's plan was for a man and a wife to enjoy each other's physical bodies in complete innocence and freedom, but the entrance of sin brought shame and the need for covering.

Protecting the purity of your marriage begins when you are still a single person. You choose to feed your spiritual and personal relationships instead of feeding lust and sensuality in yourself and others. Sensual clothes are the covering of a sensual heart. You may disagree, but there's a saying that goes, "If it looks like a duck, walks like a duck, and quacks like a duck, guess what? It's a duck!"

Dressing Facts & Effects

The purpose of this book is not to point fingers at others. We should all be looking to the Word of God. It's God's mirror and it always tells us the truth about ourselves. Any pointing going on should be done by Him, and we need to have open hearts to receive the things He points out to us.

Fair or not, the way we dress affects our influence on others, for the good or the bad. Look at David and Bathsheba. The Bible calls David "a man after God's own heart," but when he saw Bathsheba bathing on her rooftop, he fell and fell hard.

The way we dress affects our own spirits. Just think about the difference in the way you feel on Easter Sunday wearing that new outfit with the darling new spring shoes and how you feel on Saturday afternoon dressed for chores. You feel differently about yourself. And there's this crazy catch-22 that girls throw themselves in the middle of. We say we get upset when guys stare at our body parts, but if we put them out there for the world to see, how can we complain? On the one hand we want the power to know we can turn heads and draw attention, and on the other hand we feel devalued when that's what people are looking at when they're talking to us.

When we wear skirts and dresses, we feel more feminine. Most people usually treat women in dresses with more courtesy and respect. In modest dress, our spirits seem a bit meeker, a bit quieter. Perhaps when we dress like a lady we naturally act more ladylike. On a positive note, Wendy Shalit's second book on modesty, *Girls Gone Mild – Moving Away from Trashy to Classy,* indicates a trend towards modesty seems to be resurfacing.[1]

Living modestly comes down to two things: First, making a commitment to do it, and second, making the day-to-day choices that lead you down the path to the godly woman you want to be. **Who we become in the future is based on the choices we make today**—choices to either pursue God and live our lives in ways that honor Him or not.

True modesty starts below the exterior. It goes beyond hemlines, slits, and styles. It is an issue of purity in thoughts and actions that shows up in the way we dress and conduct ourselves. Modesty is a result of a surrendered heart. If you don't feel your heart is where it needs to be right now, pray like King David in Psalm 51:10: "Create in me a clean heart, O God; and renew a right spirit within me."

Saying yes to God may mean we have to say no to other things, things that may be offensive to Him or go against teachings in the Bible, but it's worth it. The good feeling modest dressing brings is better than the feeling we get when we dress for attention.

|Without modesty, beauty is lacking| and personality is not enough. Jeremiah 6:15 warns that people can do things God calls abomination and lose even the sense to blush about it. I pray God's girls never lose their ability to blush, their sense of right and wrong, shame or embarrassment. God gave us those feelings for a reason, and we don't want to become calloused or desensitized.

If you've struggled in the area of modesty, God is waiting and willing to give you grace and help, just like the father who received his prodigal son and gave him a new robe when he humbly returned to his house. Even when he walked away and made bad choices, his father loved him and watched for his return. We can't always erase the things we've done or the not-so-great choices we've made, but God can restore our virtue and dignity when we turn to Him for His grace and forgiveness.

Try This On...

Modesty is an act of worship done with humility and respect for God and others, including ourselves. It is not our salvation, but something we do because we are saved, and something that can draw others to God.

"Like moon or sunlight shining on water, making a pathway of light all the way to the horizon, so the Pure Path beckons all who would follow the Lord wholeheartedly. He calls His chosen people to a life of purity and separation, from all that would defile or make us unfit for an eternity in His holy presence.

"His call encompasses more than just clothing and outward manifestations although these cannot be ignored. He desires holiness within, springing up like an artesian well and flowing out through you into your world as a testimony to His goodness, mercy, and grace. He seeks for hidden adornments like a meek and quiet spirit, humility, and unfeigned love of your brothers and sisters in Christ, your neighbors, and His Word. He looks for those who, of their own free will, choose a life of holiness, righteousness, and godliness in this present world and prepare themselves for the eternity to come."

— Marjorie Kinnee, Rochester Hills, Michigan

Notes & Resources

Chapter 1

1. Fr. John A. Hardon, *Modern Catholic Dictionary* (Eternal Life, Bardstown, KY, 1999).

2. Hana Ali, *More than a Hero: Muhammad Ali's Life Lessons Presented Through His Daughter's Eye* (Simon and Schuster, New York, NY, May 2000).

Chapter 2

1. Gothic.Net, http://www.gothic.net/boards/showthread.php?t=28; accessed May 15, 2009.

2. Jeff Pollard, *Christian Modesty and the Public Undressing of America* (Vision Forum, Incorporated, San Antonio, TX, October 2003).

Chapter 3

1. David K. Bernard, *Essentials of Holiness* (Word Aflame Press, Hazelwood, MO, 1993).

Chapter 4

1. Noah Webster, *The American Dictionary of the English Language* (1828).

2. Wendy Shalit, *A Return to Modesty: Discovering the Lost Virtue* (Free Press, New York, 1999).

Chapter 5

1. Pollard, ibid.

2. Bernard, ibid.

3. Merril C. Tenney, *Zondervan Pictorial Encyclopedia of the Bible* (Zondervan Publishing House, Grand Rapids, MI, March 1975).

4. Merriam-Webster Online, http://www.merriam-webster.com/dictionary/CONFORM, accessed May 21, 2009.

5. Linda Y. Reed, *Subconscious Sexual Signals,* 2005.

Chapter 6

1. Modesty Survey, http://www.therebelution.com/modestysurvey, accessed May 5, 2009.

Chapter 7

1. Wendy Shalit, *Girls Gone Mild* (Random House, New York, NY, 2007).

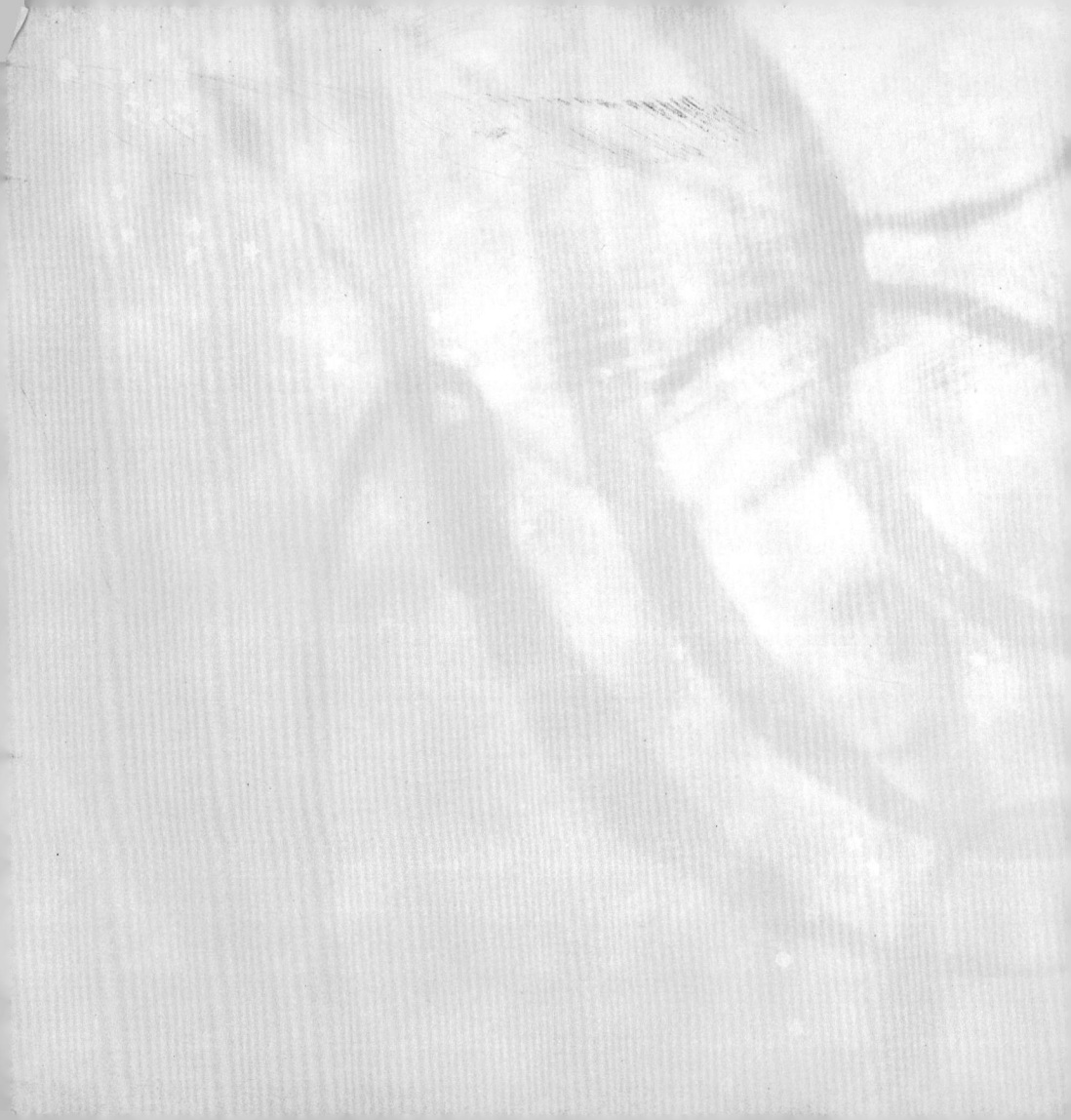